D1409130

TRIBUTE TO HER MAJESTY

Produced and Designed by
SERGE LEMOINE

Text by
DON COOLICAN

WINDWARD/SCOTT PUBLISHING

First published in Great Britain 1986 by Scott Publishing Company Limited, London, England in co. production with BBC Hulton Picture Library.

Text: Scott Publishing Company Limited, 17 Fleet Street, London, EC4Y 1AA, England.

Consultants: Manab Majunder, Gaynor Coolican.

Colour Separations by Latent Image, London, England.

Typesetting by Spectrum Typesetting Ltd., London, England.

Printed and bound by Collins, Glasgow, Scotland.

ISBN 0 7112 0437 3
SCOTT PUBLISHING COMPANY LIMITED

TRIBUTE TO HER MAJESTY

Contents

PICTURE ACKNOWLEDGEMENTS

Cover:	*SERGE LEMOINE*
Back Cover:	*BBC HULTON PICTURE LIBRARY*
Camera Press:	*36 (bottom) 41 (bottom right) 41 (top) 59 (bottom) 66 (top) 68 (bottom) – 70 – 71 (bottom). 72 (top). 73 (bottom) – 74. 75 – 84 – 85 (top). 86 (top) – 87 – 88. 89 – 90 – 92 (top) – 93 – 94. 95 – 96. 97 – 98 – 108. 109 – 110. 111 – 112. 113 – 124 – 128 – 145. 146 – 147 – 148 (top) 148 (bottom left) – 149 – 164 (top left) – 166. 167 – 204. 205 – 206. 207 – 208. 209 – 250. 251 – 260 – 263 – 273 – 279 – 285 – 286. 287 – 294. 295 – 300. 301 – 302 – 303 – 304. 305 – 306. 307 – 311 –*
Paul Cullen:	*34 (top) 35 (2) 37 (right & bottom) 38 (bottom) 41 (bottom extreme right)*
Tim Graham:	*238. 239 – 240. 241 – 242. 243 – 264. 265 – 266. 267 – 268. 269 – 270. 271*
Her Majesty's Stationery Office:	*86 (bottom)*
Rex Features:	*156 – 157*
Royal Archives, Windsor:	*34 (bottom) 38 (top) 39 (bottom) 40 (all pictures) 41 (top) 44 – 45. 46 – 47. 65 – 69 (bottom) 73 (top left) 91* *Copyright reserved. Reproduced by gracious permission of her Majesty the Queen.*
Photo Source:	*82 – 83. 244 – 245. 260 – 261*
BBC Hulton Picture Library:	*All the remaining pictures are from the BBC archives.*

Royal Line of Succession

CERDIC, first king of the West Saxons (d.534)

Crioda

CYNRIC (534-560)

CEAWIN (560-591)

Cuthwine (d.584)

Cuthwulf

Ceolwald

Cenred, under-king of Sussex (692)

Ingild (d.718), brother of King Ine

Eoppa

Eaba

Ealhmund, under-king of Kent (786)

EGBERT = Redburh

ETHELWULF = Osburh (1st wife)

ALFRED THE GREAT = Ealhswith

EDWARD = Edgiva (3rd wife)

EDMUND I = Elgiva (1st wife)

EDGAR = Elfrida (2nd wife)

ETHELRED II THE UNREADY = Elfleda (1st wife)

EDMUND II IRONSIDE = Ealdgyth

Edward Atheling the Exile = Agatha

St. Margaret = Malcolm III of Scotland

WILLIAM I (the Conqueror) = Matilda of Flanders

HENRY I = Matilda (1st wife)

Geoffrey, Count of Anjou = Matilda

HENRY II = Eleanor of Aquitaine

JOHN = Isabella of Angoulême (2nd wife)

HENRY III = Eleanor of Provence

EDWARD I = Eleanor of Castile (1st wife)

EDWARD II = Isabella of France

EDWARD III = Philippa of Hainault

John of Gaunt Duke of Lancaster = Katharine Swynford (3rd wife)

Edmund Duke of York = Isabel of Castile (1st wife)

John, Marquess of Dorset = Margaret Holland

Richard, Earl of Cambridge = Anne Mortimer

John, Beaufort, Duke of Somerset = Margaret Beauchamp

Richard, Duke of York = Cecily Neville

Edmund Tudor, Earl of Richmond = Margaret Beaufort

EDWARD IV = Elizabeth Woodville

HENRY VII = Elizabeth of York

James IV of Scotland = Margaret Tudor

HENRY VIII = Anne Boleyn (2nd wife)

ELIZABETH I

James V of Scotland = Mary of Lorraine

Mary, Queen of Scots = Henry Stuart, Lord Darnley (2nd husband)

JAMES I = Anne of Denmark

Frederick, King of Bohemia = Elizabeth Stuart

Ernest Augustus, Elector of Hanover = Sophia

GEORGE I = Sophia Dorothea of Celle

GEORGE II = Caroline of Brandenburg = Anspach

Frederick Lewis, Prince of Wales = Augusta of Saxe-Gotha

GEORGE III = Charlotte of Mecklenburg-Strelitz

Edward, Duke of Kent = Victoria of Saxe-Coburg-Saalfeld

VICTORIA = Albert of Saxe-Coburg and Gotha (Prince Consort)

EDWARD VII = Alexandra of Denmark

GEORGE V = Mary of Teck

GEORGE VI = The Lady Elizabeth Bowes-Lyon

QUEEN ELIZABETH II = The Prince Philip, Duke of Edinburgh

Charles, Prince of Wales — Prince William — Prince Henry

The Princess Anne — Master Peter Phillips — Lady Zara Phillips

The Prince Andrew

The Prince Edward

Britain's Sovereigns

William I	1066-1087
William II	1087-1100
Henry I	1100-1135
Stephen	1135-1154
Henry II	1154-1189
Richard I	1189-1199
John	1199-1216
Henry III	1216-1272
Edward I	1272-1307
Edward II	1307-1327
Edward III	1327-1377
Richard II	1377-1399
Henry IV	1399-1413
Henry V	1413-1422
Henry VI	1422-1461
Edward IV	1461-1483
Edward V	1483
Richard III	1483-1485
Henry VII	1485-1509
Henry VIII	1509-1547
Edward VI	1547-1553
Jane Grey	1553
Mary I	1553-1558
Elizabeth I	1558-1603
James I	1603-1625
Charles I	1625-1649
Commonwealth Declared 1648	
Oliver Cromwell Lord Protector	1653-1658
Richard Cromwell Lord Protector	1658-1659
Charles II	1649-1685
James II	1685-1689
William III and	1689-1702
Mary II	1689-1694
Anne	1702-1714
George I	1714-1727
George II	1727-1760
George III	1760-1820
George IV	1820-1830
William IV	1830-1837
Victoria	1837-1901
Edward VII	1901-1910
George V	1910-1936
Edward VIII	1936
George VI	1936-1952
Elizabeth II	Succeeded 1952

Today's Royal Line of Succession

1 H.R.H. The Prince of Wales (Heir Apparent)
2 H.R.H. Prince William
3 H.R.H. Prince Henry
4 H.R.H. Prince Andrew
5 H.R.H. Prince Edward
6 H.R.H. The Princess Anne
7 Master Peter Phillips
8 Lady Zara Phillips
9 H.R.H. The Princess Margaret
10 Viscount Linley
11 Lady Sarah Armstrong-Jones
12 H.R.H. The Duke of Gloucester
13 The Earl of Ulster
14 Lady Davina Windsor
15 Lady Rose Windsor
16 H.R.H. The Duke of Kent
17 The Earl of St Andrews
18 Lord Nicholas Windsor
19 Lord Frederick Windsor
20 Lady Helen Windsor

THE EARLY YEARS

CHILDHOOD DAYS

I declare before you all that my whole life, whether it be long or short, shall be devoted to your service and the service of our great Imperial Commonwealth to which we all belong H.R.H. Princess Elizabeth Alexandra Mary, at the age of twenty-one.

IT IS NOW nearly forty years since so dramatic a declaration of how she would lead her life was made by a young girl who shortly afterwards was called upon to fulfil her destiny. The Coronation of Queen Elizabeth the Second took place six years after she had made this pledge in a broadcast from South Africa, then a member of the Commonwealth.

Elizabeth was to recall later how she had made this convenant in what she called her 'salad days'. Nothing has changed in her devotion to her role in life as the years have gone by, and she now celebrates her sixtieth birthday.

So far the landmarks of her life are among the burnished milestones of the history of the Twentieth Century. She has been a major figure on the global stage since she inherited the Throne as an unworldly twenty-five-year-old thirty-four years ago. Yet when she was born her future was that of a 'minor Royal' with little chance that one day she would wear the Crown. A quirk of history changed all that.

Elizabeth was born in the early hours of April 21, 1926, at her parents' temporary home in Bruton Street in the heart of London's fashionable Mayfair. Hers was not a straightforward birth – she was delivered by Caesarian section. Her parents were the Duke and Duchess of York, who would become, reluctantly, King George the Sixth and Queen Elizabeth after the abdication of the Duke of Windsor as Heir to the Throne.

The Duke, Prince Albert George – known as 'Bertie' to his family – was the second son of King George the Fifth and Queen Mary. Bertie, as second in line to his elder brother David, Prince of Wales (later the Duke of Windsor) never expected the Crown. The Royal mother was Lady Elizabeth Bowes-Lyon who would become the first wholly British queen for centuries, and the first Scottish queen the English have ever had. Now of course she is known affectionately to the entire world as the 'Queen Mum'.

Elizabeth came from the sort of family that over the centuries has provided spouses for the sons of kings and aristocrats. Her background was one where anxious mamas made sure their daughters were of suitable charm, grace and iron-willed fibre to be chased by only the best suitors. Then, as now, though with less acreage in the gossip columns, the parents of such 'gels' pushed their laced, delicate, demure and witty – but not obviously too witty – daughters to the front of Society, hoping for the best 'catch'.

Elizabeth Angela Marguerite Bowes-Lyon – the Lady Elizabeth of Glamis – was the third daughter of the Earl and Countess of Strathmore and Kinghorne. Her father had a Scottish ancestry dating back to Robert the Bruce, King of Scotland, while her mother, Nina Cecilia, was of English stock. She was the daughter of the Reverend Charles William Cavendish -Bentinck, a cousin of the Duke of Portland. Among her ancestors was one wretched Lady Glamis who was burnt alive as a witch in Edinburgh in 1540.

The Bowes-Lyon name comes from the 18th century, when a rich County Durham industrialist, George Bowes, agreed to get the Strathmore family out of debt. The ninth earl wished to marry Bowes' daughter, Eleanor. The dowry that went with her was his entire fortune and all his estates in the North and in Hertfordshire. In exchange for the wealth and hand in marriage of such a valuable daughter the Strathmore family name of Lyon had to be changed to Bowes. After the old boy died the name quickly became Bowes-Lyon.

The Royal mother's father was a quiet, kindly, religious man. As Lord Lieutenant of Forfar, he lived the classic role of an Anglo-Scottish gentleman of his day, being mainly concerned with shooting, cricket and forestry.

His wife had the greatest influence on their youngest daughter, Lady Elizabeth Bowes-Lyon. The Countess of Strathmore was a strait-laced lady interested in embroidery and music. She was so accomplished musically that she could attend a concert, return home, go straight to the piano, and play the pieces from memory. She is said to have been a lively woman with a great sense of humour...qualities which her daughter inherited in abundance.

Much of Lady Elizabeth's childhood was spent at Glamis, the old Scottish castle dating back to the Fourteenth Century. It was here that the teenager discovered interests which lasted throughout her life: she learned to play cricket and tennis, developed into an accomplished gardener, and became skilful at fly fishing.

She startled London and Scottish society when she came on the social scene. Contemporary pictures show her as an impish-eyed, petite (5 ft. 2 in.) beauty, trim of waist and with gentle mouth and soft jawline. Her blue eyes were described as brilliant and she was said to have a lovely skin and complexion. Her peaches-and-cream look – inherited by her daughter – has been the envy of most women throughout her life. By the time she made her debut at court she was already beginning to turn heads as a striking, dark-haired 19-year-old. Drawing-room gossip of the time praised her as being irresistible to men.

She had the reputation of being full of high spirits, one of the best ballroom dancers of the early 1920's and her company was generally thought to be great fun. She was once praised as 'a sweet-faced, pretty and gentle-natured girl'. Her entry into the heart of Royal circles came through being on various committees of the Girl Guides. Princess Mary (later Lady Harewood) was also a keen Guide, and befriended the Scottish lass.

Princess Mary the only daughter of King George V and Queen Mary invited her to Buckingham Palace, where she soon attracted the attentions of the two eldest of the four Royal sons, 26-year-old David and 25-year-old Albert. When Bertie began pursuing Lady Elizabeth Bowes-Lyon his family thought he was doomed to disappointment: 'You'll be a lucky fellow if she accepts you,' warned King George. Though Albert was young, slim and good-looking, he was shy and had an embarrassing stammer.

Elizabeth had no shortage of suitors, and when the Prince first proposed to her she refused him. Bertie continued to pay court in London and in Scotland. Slowly he wore away her doubts, and after two years of persistent courtship, was able to telegraph to his parents, *'All right. Bertie.'*

'Bertie is supremely happy,' Queen Mary wrote after the bride-to-be had been to Sandringham and Bertie had successfully found himself a wife. From the moment of his marriage, Bertie became the King's favourite son. George mellowed from an earlier harsh attitude towards his family: 'My father was frightened of his mother, I was frightened of my father, and I am damned well going to see to it that my children are frightened of me.' His sons were said to be petrified of him.

Bertie, the first of the brothers to be married, received fatherly approval. 'The better I know and the more I see of your dear little wife,' the King wrote to him shortly after the wedding, 'the more charming I think she is and everyone fell in love with her here.' Even Queen Mary, as cold a parent as her husband, began to soften. She became devoted to her first daughter-in-law, whom she described as 'the pretty Strathmore girl.'

The new Duchess of York – as Elizabeth became after the wedding – and Bertie, who took up the title of Duke of York as an alternative to Prince Albert, made their first 'official' home White Lodge, a rambling old house in Richmond Park, eight miles south-west from Buckingham Palace. They preferred to be nearer their friends in the 'smart-set' quarter of London, however. This was the age of the 'flapper', 1920s wildness and nightclub life that Elizabeth and Bertie flung themselves into as young society leaders of their day.

They spent most of their newly-wed days at the London home of Elizabeth's parents, No. 17 Bruton Street, W1, a fashionable thoroughfare linking Berkeley Square with Bond Street. It was here, three years after their wedding, that the Yorks had their first child. The fact that she was a girl disappointed King George, who had hoped for his first grandchild to be a boy.

Apart from having two surgeons in attendance at the difficult birth, the 26-year-old duchess also had on hand the Home Secretary of the day, Sir William Joynson Hicks. One of the Government's senior Ministers was present because of a tradition going back almost 300 years. This was an antiquated requirement, completely out of place in the Twentieth Century, but insisted upon following the wrangling at the time Mary of Modena, consort of the maligned Roman Catholic James II. She was believed to be incapable of childbearing, but had a son in July 1688. Shocked at the thought of another Papist on the Throne, the Protestant Whigs falsely denounced the child as a foundling smuggled into the Queen's bedchamber in a warming-pan.

Since that time it became customary for someone responsible to Parliament to guarantee the legitimate claims of a possible Heir to the Throne. Queen Elizabeth II did not have to submit herself to this scrutiny when giving birth to Prince Charles and her other children in a more enlightened era.

With Parliamentary 'approval' the baby who would one day be Queen arrived and an official announcement was made: *'Her Royal Highness the Duchess of York was safely delivered of a Princess (at 2.40) this morning. Both mother and daughter are doing well.'*

King George and Queen Mary had left instructions that they were to be told straight away if there were any developments at Bruton Street. In the small hours of Wednesday, April 21, duty equerry Captain Reginald Seymour obeyed orders and roused the King and Queen to tell them the good news. 'We were awakened at 4.00 a.m.,' wrote Queen Mary, at Windsor, 'and Reggie Seymour informed us that darling Elizabeth had got a daughter at 2.40. Such a relief and joy.'

That afternoon Mary and George arrived at Bruton Street to be told that the young mother was asleep. 'We saw the baby,' Queen Mary wrote, delighted with her first grand-daughter. 'A little darling with a lovely complexion and fair hair.' Other first visitors described the new arrival as 'possessing fair hair', 'large, dark-lashed blue eyes', and 'tiny ears set close to a well shaped head'. The Queen also thought the child was enchanting, but she wished the baby was 'more like your little mother.'

BERTIE GUSHED like any other proud father in a letter to his mother a few days later. He wrote: 'You don't know what a tremendous joy it is to Elizabeth and me to have our little girl. We always wanted a child to make our happiness complete, and now that it has happened, it seems so wonderful and strange. I am so proud of Elizabeth at this moment after all she has gone through during the last few days, and I am so thankful that everything has happened as it should and so successfully. I do hope you and Papa are as delighted as we are to have a grand-daughter, or would you have sooner had a grandson? May I say I hope you won't spoil her when she gets a bit older.'

Newspapers the next day were not as ecstatic as the princely father, though. They gave the Royal Birth second place to developments in the General Strike. For the future Queen arrived in the middle of industrial strife; troops were encamped not far from her cot in Hyde Park to cope with the emergency.

On May 3 the country was thrown into chaos by the nationwide strike, and the whole of Britain was virtually paralysed for ten days.

Another reason why the newspapers were not dutifully delighted was that there was no reason why the birth of a daughter to the Duke and Duchess of York should have any special significance. She was not in the direct line of succession. Once her Uncle David, the Prince of Wales, had married and began a family, and indeed once her own parents had bred a few male children, she would be a completely outside runner as a possible Heir to the Throne.

Prince Albert ranked below his elder brother in Royal precedence. Therefore it seemed far-fetched in 1926 to link this new baby Princess with the Throne. Her only chance of becoming a queen in the future was probably as the wife of some foreign king. For the time being, though, she was third in the Order of Succession.

As the duchess recovered from the strains of a difficult confinement, she and Bertie settled down to discuss what names they should choose for their daughter. They wanted 'Elizabeth' as a link with the mother, but they were worried that the King – a final arbiter on these matters – would not approve.

Prince Albert wrote to his father: 'Such a nice name. I am sure there will be no muddle over two Elizabeths in the family and there has been no one of that name in your family for a long time. Elizabeth of York sounds so nice, too.' King George replied with his approval for all the names chosen. 'Alexandra' remembered his own mother and 'Mary' complimented his wife. As for 'Elizabeth', he said he thought this was 'such a pretty name.'

'I have heard from Bertie,' he told Queen Mary. 'He mentions Elizabeth Alexandra Mary. I quite approve and will tell him so.'

The christening took place in the private chapel of Buckingham Palace on May 29. It was an essentially quiet family affair, performed by the Archbishop of York and attended by parents, grandparents and godparents. Traditional 'Royal Water' from the River Jordan was used from the gold lily font made for the christening of Vicky, Princess Royal, in 1840. 'Of course poor baby cried,' Queen Mary wrote afterwards.

The crying baby was dressed in the cream satin robe overlaid with Honiton lace that had been worn by nearly all of Queen Victoria's children.

The Duchess of York breast-fed her baby for the first month, then, having to resume official duties, handed her into the arms of Mrs. Clara Knight, who had been her own nanny. With the help of a nurserymaid she fed, dressed and exercised the new baby Princess and, twice a day, presented her in a clean dress to her adoring parents.

When the little girl woke up crying in the night it was the nursery staff who went to comfort her. Mrs. Knight's Christian name was Clara, but this defeated her charge, who could only manage 'Alla' – and this remained the name by which Princess Elizabeth knew her. She was an old-fashioned nanny, a family retainer in the traditional style, whose whole life was her work, welcoming the role of surrogate mother put on her by her employers, delighting in the challenge of coping with everything, and scarcely ever taking a holiday or day off.

For most couples the following few months would be an idyllic period of settling down together as a family with their first child. Not for the Yorks, however. The baby was barely eight months old when the Duke and Duchess were sent to Australia and New Zealand on an official tour.

The tour was to be their first major public duty together in the Empire – but they had to abandon their first child in London for six months in the hands of Nanny Knight. The Duchess trusted Mrs. Knight, but like any first-time mother she worried over leaving her child behind.

In the weeks before departure the Duchess spent as many hours as possible with Princess Elizabeth. A friend visiting her at this time found the baby 'sitting up by herself in the middle of the huge Chesterfield, like a white fluff of thistle-down. The baby is always good, she has the sweetest air of complete serenity.'

When she and Bertie were leaving home to board the battleship *Renown* for their journey across the globe the young mum went back twice to kiss her baby after she had placed Elizabeth in the nurse's arms in the hallway. On the way to the railway station from Bruton Street the chauffeur had to circle Grosvenor Gardens twice so that Elizabeth could recover her composure before facing the crowds.

Throughout the tour cables were sent each week to the anxious parents giving news of their daughter. A photographer took pictures of the child so that they would miss as little as possible of their daughter's progress. These little touches helped, but how many mothers could endure the first few months of their child's life in this way? 'We are not supposed to be human,' said the Duchess.

When they returned from their first overseas tour Elizabeth was reunited with a daughter who had grown twice the size while she was away. The baby was greeted with hugs and kisses at Buckingham Palace.

Elizabeth made her first appearance on the balcony of Buckingham Palace when she was just thirteen months old. Shielded by one of Queen Mary's parasols, she was carried out in her mother's arms, to the acclaim of the excited crowds below. The Royal pair, united as a proper family at last, left the Palace later in the afternoon to go to a new home, 145 Piccadilly, where they were to spend ten blissful years.

Number 145, four doors away from Apsley House, the 'Iron' Duke of Wellington's mansion, had been prepared for the Duke and Duchess while they were away. Until the lease had been acquired for the Duke the house had stood empty for several years. It was built in 1795 from designs by the famous architects and designers, the Adam brothers . . . a tall, four-storeyed building faced with grey stone, which no longer exists.

The Queen today remembers this as one of the happiest periods in her life. She was brought up in a warm family circle. The Victorian habit of banning the children to the nursery and rarely seeing them until they could either shoot or ride had long since died by the time of her own childhood.

Because of the loving atmosphere she remembered with her parents, she arranged that there would be no barriers of governesses and nannies between herself and her own children when they came on the scene years afterwards. Elizabeth had a nursery on the top floor of the house packed with hundreds of toys sent by well-wishers from all over Britain and the Commonwealth.

Life at 145 was described as follows by a Royal courtier: 'When Princess Elizabeth's nurse, descending to the morning room or the drawing room, says in her quiet tones, 'I think it is bed time now, Elizabeth,' there are no pouting protests, just a few last joyous skips and impromptu dance steps, a few last minute laughs at mummy's delicious bed time jokes, and then Princess Elizabeth's hand slips into her nurse's hand, and the two go off gaily together across the deep chestnut pile of the hall carpet to the accommodating lift, which in two seconds has whisked them up to the familiar dear domain which is theirs to hold and to share.'

The house had no private garden but shared with its neighbours a communal area of lawn and bushes known as Hamilton Gardens. Here the Princess played games, sometimes joined by her father. In the upstairs nursery were the 'stables' for the collection of rocking-horses, which required 'exercise', 'grooming' and feeding'. Every evening she would change their saddles and harness before going to bed.

It was during these happy 'toddler days' that the childhood name that has stuck with her among her own family came about. She could not pronounce 'Elizabeth' properly so she became 'Lilibet', a name she is known as today to her mother and sister. She was officially 're-christened' Lilibet by the King, who was so charmed by her stumbling attempts to handle her name. She called him 'grandpa England' and she was thoroughly spoiled by the man whose own children had been terrified of him.

On one occasion, when she was four years old, Elizabeth was in the grounds of Buckingham Palace and passed a sentry, who presented arms. Wishing to see whether he would do it again, she retraced her steps. Once more he saluted. This amusement continued for twenty minutes. By the time an officer arrived on his rounds the sentry was exhausted. The officer fetched a nurse who took away the Princess before the sentry collapsed.

George used to take her to Bognor Regis, the Sussex seaside resort, favoured by the King because he enjoyed the bracing air. It was there that Elizabeth spent many happy days playing sandcastles with her grandfather while he was recovering from a severe illness.

During November 1928, while attending the Armistice Day ceremony at the Cenotaph, King George caught a chill which he neglected. Within days he lay seriously ill with septicaemia. Bertie, who was hunting in the Midlands with the Pytchley, quickly returned to London. Brother David, Heir to the Throne, touring East Africa, was also warned of the gravity of his father's condition.

Christmas at Sandringham, the Norfolk Royal estate, was cancelled and for the first time the King had to forego one of his favourite pilgrimages. Princess Elizabeth was allowed to stay up late to listen to the carol singers on Christmas Eve, and when she heard 'Glad tidings of great joy I bring to you and all mankind', she called out excitedly, 'I know who Old Man Kind is!' To her young mind it seemed natural that so many people should be singing so enthusiastically about her grandfather!

After a successful operation on his lung, George went to convalesce at Bognor. Lilibet, whom the King adored, went to stay with him in the hope it would help his recovery. When he continued writing his diary, it was to 'our sweet little grandchild' that he often referred. She was then three years old.

'G delighted to see her,' wrote Queen Mary in her diary. As King George V recovered, he was able to appear in public on the seafront with his grand-daughter. There was great cheering. George nodded his head in a grandfatherly fashion and the little Princess responded by waving brightly.

When the King got back to London he kept a regular contact with his grand-daughter. The Princess took to drawing back the curtains of the front windows at 145 Piccadilly in the hope that she could see her grandfather at Buckingham Palace.

Her father would lift her on to the window-sill so that she could wave, while the King, in the Palace looked at her through binoculars from half a mile away across Green Park. She was shamelessly spoilt by George: when staying at Windsor, he would let her sweep the food off his plate to feed a pet or go down on his hands and knees to search for her hairslide under the sofa.

Summer holidays with her mother and father usually consisted of simple picnics or paddling on the sands at Dunan Bay, near Montrose in Forfarshire. Elizabeth loved being with dogs and horses and these seemed to be the happiest moments of her day. Christmas was often spent at Sandringham. George was once seen on the floor being led by the beard by his grandchild, the 'sweet little Lilibet', as they played horse and groom there.

At 145 Piccadilly, the Princess saw her parents first thing in the morning, when she crept into their bedroom, and last thing at night when they took part in the fun and games of bathtime. As she grew older, she was included in their entertaining, both personal and official, in much the same way as her mother had taken part in the social life of her parents.

Royal status did impose problems, however. Just across the road from 145 Piccadilly, Green Park seemed the perfect place for outings in the pram. Unfortunately it was also very public, and after several times finding herself besieged by well-intentioned but worrying crowds, Nanny Knight was forced to abandon these excursions. The Princess had to be content with the gardens behind the walls of Buckingham Palace.

Four years after the birth of Princess Elizabeth, the Yorks' second child came along. In view of what happened in a stormy later life that is now so well publicised, it might seem almost appropriate that Princess Margaret Rose was born on a day of thunder and lightning.

The Duchess gave birth to Margaret at Glamis Castle on August 21, 1930. She was the first member of the Royal Family to be born in Scotland for more than 300 years. While the weary mother wanted to recuperate in peace, the local pipe band celebrated the event noisily by marching about the neighbourhood with a small army of villagers, who rounded off the day with a bonfire on a nearby hill. Fortunately the Duchess liked the sound of the pipes.

Confident that the child would be a boy, Elizabeth and Bertie had given little thought to girls' names, but within a week they had decided that their daughter should be called Ann Margaret. The King did not like the name Ann and would not even approve changing to Margaret Ann.

The Duchess pleaded with Queen Mary for her help. She wrote to her: 'I am very anxious to call her Ann Margaret as I think that Ann of York sounds pretty and Elizabeth and Ann go so well together. I wonder what you think? Lots of people have suggested Margaret, but it has no family links really on either side.'

George would not be moved so eventually another letter, this time of capitulation, was sent. 'Bertie and I have decided now to call our little daughter 'Margaret Rose', instead of M. Ann, as Papa does not like Ann. I hope you like it. I think that it is very pretty together.' Sister Elizabeth's response to the new arrival was: 'I've got a baby sister, Margaret Rose, and I'm going to call her Bud. She's not a real rose yet, is she? She's only a bud.'

There were some suggestions in Royal and political circles that Margaret and Elizabeth should now hold equal rank in the line of accession. George would not have this. Shortly after the christening, the King announced the order as he saw it. Heir to the throne, David, Prince of Wales, followed (subject to change if he should have children) by the Duke of York. Next in line was Princess Elizabeth while Margaret Rose occupied fourth place ahead of the King's two younger sons, the Duke of Gloucester and Prince George, later Duke of Kent. If Bertie and Elizabeth of York should have a son, that would alter the pecking order.

After the arrival of Margaret, there were plans afoot that would have given the future Queen Elizabeth a Canadian upbringing. It was suggested that the Duke of York go to Ottawa as the next Governor-General. It would have been a highly popular move if the Yorks had lived in Canada with their two little girls.

The King's advisers, Sir Clive Wigram and Lord Stamfordham, both approved the prospect, but it was disallowed by Mr. J.H. Thomas, the Dominions' Secretary of State in the Labour Cabinet, much to the Duchess's relief.

One of the most significant results of the younger sister coming on the scene for Elizabeth was that she developed a relationship more strongly than before with Margaret MacDonald who had worked as under-nurse to Mrs. Knight since the Princess was a few months old.

'Alla' as Mrs. Knight was affectionately known, had to concentrate on the new baby, so Princess Elizabeth moved closer to Miss MacDonald. Miss MacDonald was to become known affectionately to Elizabeth as 'Bobo' and she stayed alongside her Royal charge all her life, as confidante, adviser and dresser.

Lilibet still remained the favourite of George V. The Countess of Airlie, Lady-in-Waiting to Queen Mary, recorded: 'Lilibet always came first in his affections. He used to play with her – a thing I never saw him do with his own children – and loved to have her with him.'

Lady Airlie gave Elizabeth a housemaid's set for Christmas, including the usual dustpan-and-brush. She then noticed the 'resultant passion for housework' that swept over the nursery of 145 Piccadilly. The young Elizabeth's habits were as orderly as her father's and grandfather's. This addiction to tidiness was said later to have been a burden to herself and a joke to her sister.

At night instead of throwing her shoes under one chair and her clothes on another, she would arrange them meticulously more than once before going to sleep. Her sister and governess laughed her out of the habit. She stored a box with neatly rolled ribbons saved from chocolate boxes and pieces of smooth folded coloured paper. Nothing was wasted. She kept a list of her presents received at Christmas.

Eventually life for the two girls became too public. If they wanted to go for a walk or just play among flowers and trees or feed the ducks, like other children, they had to go among staring crowds. The two Princesses became such public property that passengers would go on the top deck of buses to look down into the back garden of 145.

By this stage the Royal parents realised they must find somewhere more private outside London, although Number 145 was the house that the Duchess still regarded as the first home of her own. She made the atmosphere one of home: double-glazed windows – an innovation at that time – hushed the passing traffic, and it was a house of pleasant sounds. A Georgian clock chimed a carillon of sixteen bells, and canaries sang near a garden door.

THEY CHOSE as a country retreat the Royal Lodge in Windsor Great Park, a house once occupied by the Prince Regent in the early Nineteenth Century. It was in a bad state of repair and the gardens overgrown, but the Yorks grabbed the chance of taking it over, like any other young couple who wanted to create their second home.

The Duchess was enraptured by the possibilities of the dilapidated house and wilderness of a garden. The Duke was less enthusiastic. A lot of work needed to be done, but he was none the less grateful to his father for giving it to them and pleased for his wife. She knew that the children would be excited at the prospect of a house with such a big garden in which to play.

'It is too kind of you to have offered us Royal Lodge,' the Duke wrote to his father, who replied that he was pleased they liked it but hoped they would call it 'THE Royal Lodge, by which name it had been known ever since George IV built it in the early 1800s. There can be any number of Royal Lodges, but only one known as The Royal Lodge.' The Duke stuck to his father's wishes, but over the years the prefix has been dropped and plain Royal Lodge it is.

The Duchess adored the privacy and solitude of the grounds and saw the possibilities of restoring and improving the house itself. 'Having seen it I think it will suit us admirably,' the Duke reported to the King. The King replied, 'I am so pleased to hear that both you and Elizabeth liked The Royal Lodge and would like to live there.'

The building and grounds not only became a weekend retreat but their favourite house as Mother Elizabeth jumped into the task of being a country-wife and home-maker, choosing furniture, picking curtains, stocking her kitchen, ordering a coat of fresh paint here and new wallpaper for there. It might have been a bit too chintzy for modern tastes, but she turned a neglected old dwelling into a snug hideaway of domestic bliss. Making the place habitable took them more than a year.

The Royal Lodge became the Yorks' favourite residence. The centrepiece of the house was a great banqueting salon dating from the Regency. Under a ceiling twenty feet high this room measured forty-eight feet by almost thirty feet. By comparison the rest of the house was modest in proportions.

Two wings were later added by the Duke and Duchess – one to provide bedrooms, bathrooms and sitting rooms for themselves, and the other to form the nursery and accommodation for guests. Servants' quarters were built above the garage, and in the grounds an open-air swimming pool. Here the York children grew up in a family environment that the present Queen remembers well and has tried to create for her own children.

The entire family had to 'muck-in' and sort out the garden, which was a disordered mess of weeds and thorn bushes. Elizabeth and Margaret were given their own special part to work on, though neither of them developed the same enthusiasm for horticulture that their mother shows to this day. When the Duke expanded the garden of Royal Lodge from fifteen to ninety acres, everyone joined in to clear the wilderness.

One weekend the King and Queen arrived to be confronted by a dishevelled Princess Elizabeth pushing a wheelbarrow. Solemnly they allowed themselves to be conducted to a newly planted tree, beneath which was to be found her father wielding a pair of secateurs.

Windsor was where Elizabeth's 'doggie' lineage began, when those famous corgis began to enter the scene. The first of the long line was introduced – Rozavel Golden Eagle, known to the family as 'Cookie'. The Duchess had grown up with dogs around her and she thought her children should have their company, too.

Elizabeth and Margaret and their parents lived like any other family at Windsor. There was laughter and fun away from servants. The mother could cook, in her own kitchen, simple meals that did not have the usual formality of banquets. There was a nursery where the Duchess would read the girls' bed-time stories, and later, when they were old enough, she taught them to read.

The Royal mother insisted that the upbringing of the children should be like that of any normal, though affluent, family.

Sometimes the Prince of Wales, 'Uncle David', called to take part in nursery games such as Snap, Happy Families and Racing Demon. A popular pastime was a game called Winnie-the-Pooh. The Duchess had read from the story book of that name, so David and his nieces enacted the characters in mime.

She taught Elizabeth to read via a literary diet of the Bible and fairy stories, such as *'Alice In Wonderland', 'Black Beauty', 'At the Back of the North Wind', Peter Pan'* and anything about horses and dogs.

The Duchess also had to take on the role of preparing Elizabeth for her Royal future. This involved schooling her in how to greet various persons 'of rank' she would meet in the course of her life. Elizabeth would enter the room where the child was playing and announce herself as perhaps a visiting king, prime minister or bishop to test her on the correct responses.

All of us who have admired the way in which the Royals can stand seemingly for hours without fidgeting must puzzle how on earth they manage it. The answer is that from childhood they spend ever increasing periods practising standing perfectly still. The Duchess trained both her daughters in this difficult 'art' – and most of us know how hard it is to get a child to keep still!

In their father's eyes, his daughters were both 'wonderful and strange.' Happy though Elizabeth and her sister were in each other's company, they realized very early, however, the restrictions imposed upon them. Watching at a distance other children at play was to be reminded that others led lives which were without red tape and ceremony, all so much a part of a Royal existence.

So, thrown inevitably as they were into each other's exclusive company. the two Princesses nurtured a strong bond of love and friendship. There was, occasionally, a certain amount of rivalry which ended in a fight. Such as when Margaret might pluck the elastic of her sister's hat, or Elizabeth would pinch Margaret, who would retaliate with a kick.

Elizabeth was basically a good, sweet-natured child, but she was capable of occasional rebellion, as when she upturned an inkwell on her head to break the tedium of a French lesson.

The less violent part of growing up took place in what must have been every little girl's dream – a child size, two-storey thatched cottage in the grounds of the Lodge. It was a complete home scaled down in every detail – furniture, kitchen equipment, doors and windows and ceilings – to juvenile proportions. This was a gift from the people of Wales so it was called *Y Bwthyn Bach Tô Gwellt* (The little thatched cottage).

Here the Princesses could play 'houses' in a real house. This included inviting Mummy and Daddy for tea-parties served at a knee high table just big enough for adults to squeeze their legs under.

The Princesses could do make-believe chores, and Elizabeth made the most of the little house to develop housewifely skills, though there was little chance that she would ever need them.

The Duchess was keen to send Elizabeth to school when she reached the age of seven, but the King put his foot down. She was third in line to the Throne and, though her accession did not seem very likely, Heirs to the Throne must always be educated at home. The answer was to appoint a Royal governess who would eventually oversee the lessons of both Princesses and every aspect of the girls' upbringing.

Chosen for this role was a young Scotswoman, Miss Marion Crawford. She had trained as a teacher in Edinburgh and intended to make her life's work among deprived children, but before settling down to her vocation she took a temporary job teaching the children of two families near her home at Dunfermline.

One of her employers was Lady Rose Leveson-Gower, sister to the Duchess of York, and it was through Lady Rose that the Duke and Duchess came to hear of her.

In later years Miss Crawford, or 'Crawfie' as she became known, was to upset the Royal Family because of her revelations about what went on behind the Palace gates. Much of the life of the young Elizabeth has come to light as a result of what she wrote.

On first meeting the Yorks, the Scots lassie found it 'obvious that they were devoted to each other and very much in love.' According to Miss Crawford, 'It was a couple of very spoiled and difficult people I somehow visualised as I travelled South, for already the papers had produced odd stories about these Royal children. I was more than convinced that my month's trial would stop at the end of the month, and that I should soon be home again.' She stayed sixteen years.

Crawfie had Elizabeth from nine to six each day, but her out-of-school life remained in the care of Alla and the under-nurse, Margaret MacDonald, who shared a bedroom with the Princess. When Crawfie arrived, Margaret was only two and not old enough for lessons.

Crawfie took to heart the Duke's worry that his daughters should have a lively childhood, and introduced them to gloriously grubby games of hide-and-seek. When in London they began to venture further afield into Hyde Park, but though the Princesses would gaze wistfully at the other children, they were not encouraged to make friends with them. Crawfie thought this was a pity. She arranged dancing classes or swimming lessons to help them mix with other children.

While living in the centre of London, after the peace of Windsor, they became more conscious of being cut off from the bustling world outside. They would look out of the nursery windows at the top of the house to watch the buses rolling past and ask their governess about the real world beyond their home.

Crawfie managed to open up their lives a little with occasional forays. A memorable day was their first ride on an underground train at Tottenham Court Road to have tea at the YMCA. 'Tea out of thick cups, other people's bread and butter, tea you paid for with money, these were wonderful treats,' wrote Miss Crawford in her memoirs.

Another jaunt was to ride on the top deck of a bus so that they could look down into other people's gardens. These adventures had to come to an end when the IRA began to be active in London in the Thirties.

On Friday afternoons the family piled into a car and went down to Royal Lodge. There would still be work to do, a morning spent going over the previous week's lessons with Miss Crawford, but there was also riding before lunch and then more riding or games in the garden or park with the Duke and Duchess in the afternoon.

According to Crawfie, lunch was always taken with the Duke and Duchess whenever they were at home. Tea was occasionally taken with guests of their own age, but often with Uncle David.

High spot of the day was bath time. When both girls were splashing about, the parents would go upstairs and join in the fun. The party would move on to the bedroom with pillow fights, squeaks and giggles. 'Then, arm in arm, the young parents would go downstairs, heated and dishevelled and frequently damp... The children called to them as they went, until the final door closed, "Goodnight, Mummy, goodnight, Papa!"', remembered Miss Crawford.

Crawfie also revealed how she set a programme for the formal education of a future Queen. Half an hour's religious instructions began the week at 9.30 every Monday morning. Following mornings always began with an arithmetic lesson, then history, English grammar, geography, literature or writing. Mme. Montaudon-Smith taught French, while Mlle. Georgina Guérin gave French conversation during the holidays.

After three lessons of half an hour each, there was a break between eleven and twelve o'clock for a drink of orange juice and games. She then had an hour's rest, during which she read to herself, or Crawfie read aloud.

On Mondays after lunch Miss Betty Vacani taught dancing, on Tuesdays there were singing classes at the Knightsbridge home of the Countess of Cavan, on Wednesdays drawing, on Thursdays a music lesson, and on Friday afternoon there was the family exodus to Windsor. On Saturday mornings, from half past nine until eleven o'clock, the Princess did a résumé of the week's work and some general reading.

The Duchess had insisted that history and geography were more important than arithmetic.

As a result Elizabeth never did progress very far with mathematics, though intelligent and quick to learn in other subjects.

This difficulty with figures was inherited by Prince Charles, who had a struggle getting his maths up to scratch when he joined the Royal Air Force as a pilot.

King George's educational demands were simpler: 'For goodness sake teach Margaret and Lilibet to write a decent hand, that's all I ask you. None of my children could write properly. They all do it exactly the same way. I like a hand with some character in it.'

Although she never made friends again with her former charges after being so indiscreet with her writings in the late 1940s, Crawfie had only the fondest memories of her days with the Royals.

She wrote: 'No one ever had employers who interfered so little. I often had the feeling that the Duke and Duchess, most happy in their own married life, were not over-concerned with the higher education of their daughters. They wanted most for them a really happy childhood, with lots of pleasant memories stored up against the days that might come and, later, happy marriages.'

Both Elizabeth and Margaret became accomplished in the social arts befitting Princesses. Singing and dancing came very easily to them. Elizabeth began riding at the age of four and by six had dispensed with the leading rein. Her teacher was the Duke's stud groom, Owen, who became such a hero to her that on one occasion when her father was asked a question he replied impatiently, 'Don't ask me, ask Owen. Who am I to make suggestions?'

Owen was charmed by his pupil: 'Words fail me to thoroughly explain how very nice Princess Elizabeth really is,' he wrote in a letter.

In May 1935, King George V and Queen Mary celebrated the Silver Jubilee of their reign. The Yorks and Princess Elizabeth joined in much of the public appearances that were part of the festivities. She endeared herself even more to the old monarch. The King said to an old friend, Lady Algy Gordon-Lennox: 'I pray to God that my eldest son will never marry and that nothing will come between Bertie and Lilibet and the Throne.'

In the New Year of 1936, the King took to his bed at Sandringham and confessed to feeling 'rotten' in his diary of Friday, January 17. Most of the houses guests disappeared, though the few who were left sat through a film.

The Queen took the Princesses out for a walk. It was snowing as she explained that their grandfather was very ill. Princess Elizabeth went to say goodbye to him as he sat propped up in bed. It was a first experience of the approach of death, and Elizabeth looked very unhappy when she left for home with her younger sister.

In the early hours of January 20, 1936 King George V died, rather sooner than even his doctors had feared. Queen Mary rose to her feet at the moment when her husband's life had gone and kissed the hand of her eldest son. At five minutes to midnight on that day, Uncle David, aged forty-one and carefree, was Edward VIII, the new King. He was to reign for 327 days and then abdicate.

Queen Mary recorded, 'At five to twelve my darling husband passed peacefully away – my children were angelic.'

The body of George V lay in state for five days at Westminster Hall, and on the last night before his funeral his four sons stood watch at each corner of the catafalque. On a cold, gloomy morning six days later, the coffin was borne on a gun carriage to Paddington Station, then taken by train to Windsor where the funeral took place in St. George's Chapel. The new King remained a little apart from the rest of his family during the day's activities. No one knew then that uppermost in his mind was what he was going to do about Mrs. Wallis Simpson, the American divorcee with whom he was hopelessly in love. A King besotted with a commoner, who could never be his queen.

Although, as a ten-year-old, Elizabeth was not aware of what was going on, the events of the next twelve months were to put the very future of the British Monarchy in jeopardy and change irrevocably the course of her own life.

His 'playboy' world was not their world, but Uncle David was a welcome visitor who amused the two Princesses with his natural frivolity. He was always such fun and he enjoyed being in a family atmosphere that he, by the age of 42, had never managed to create for himself.

The British public did not know of the rumours that were being printed abroad, though Elizabeth and Bertie could see this trouble brewing from the very start of Edward's relationship with the divorcee from Baltimore. They feared the final outcome because there could be no suggestion of a King marrying a divorced woman and remaining King.

It was a hurtful time, in which the Duchess feared Bertie and herself and the children could come out the losers. By all accounts the Queen Mother did not approve of Mrs. Simpson and even today the whole business is something she will not discuss, even with her most intimate friends.

When her husband had to shoulder unexpected kingship, she had to lay aside the private life they both valued so much. She has always felt also that Bertie's life was probably shortened as a result of being burdened with the responsibilities laid upon him by the Abdication.

The Royal Family had hoped the Mrs. Simpson affair was an infatuation that would pass, just as Uncle David's other women in the past had faded.

The King was dead – and it had to be long live the King Edward VIII – even though he wanted to marry a divorced commoner, and a foreigner to boot.

Soon after he became King, Edward began to lose interest in the job, especially when he began to realise that it was the Government that was ruling the country, and not him. He did not bother to keep up with Cabinet papers and peformed few public appearances. His entire life was centred on Wallis Simpson.

The crisis over Mrs. Simpson went on at a stormy pace throughout the summer and autumn of 1936. On November 17, King Edward broke the news about his plan to marry Mrs. Simpson. 'Bertie was so much taken aback by my news that in his shy way he could not bring himself to express his innermost feelings at the time,' Edward, when 'demoted' to the Duke of Windsor, recalled in his memoirs later.

ELIZABETH'S FATHER spent the next ten days pleading with his elder brother to see sense, without success. When his brother abdicated, Bertie was appalled. 'This can't be happening to me,' he protested when a servant correctly addressed him as 'Your Majesty'. He said miserably to his cousin Lord Mountbatten, 'This is terrible, Dickie, I never wanted this to happen. I'm quite unprepared for it... I've never seen a State paper. I'm only a Naval officer. It's the only thing I know about.' He wept in front of his mother.

When the news was broken to Elizabeth – now at eleven years old, first in line to the Throne – that her father was King and the entire family would be moving to Buckingham Palace, she said incredulously, 'You mean *for ever?*'

But a life at the Palace it was going to be from now on. An indication of the change in the family status came after Bertie returned from his public proclamation as King George VI.

According to Crawfie, again, she explained to Elizabeth and Margaret that he was King of England. 'When the King returned, both little girls swept him a beautiful curtsey. I think perhaps nothing that had occurred had brought the change in his condition to him as clearly as this did. He stood for a moment touched and taken aback. Then he stooped and kissed them both warmly.'

The new Royal parents and children left 145 Piccadilly in the words of young Elizabeth 'for ever'. To the Princesses, the Palace was virtually unknown territory. They had been taken there on private visits and on a few ceremonial occasions, but it had never been a place in which they could wander where they pleased.

One advantage of the move, though, was that the Princesses could now have ample opportunities to play outside without crowds of onlookers. They had what amounted to their own private garden.

The Royal apartments were on the first floor, overlooking Green Park in one direction and the garden in the other. On the floor above were the nurseries. Here the Princesses lived, high enough to see over the Victoria Memorial and along the Mall. A perfect spot for viewing the Changing of the Guard each morning in the forecourt below.

The two sisters excitedly, and noisily, explored the long corridors of the nursery floor. 'It was as though the place had been dead for years and had suddenly come alive,' said one member of staff.

When selecting a new schoolroom with Crawfie, the King, remembering the gloomy schoolroom of his own childhood, wanted to avoid a similar unpleasant environment for his daughters. A bright room overlooking the garden and the lake was chosen. Here Elizabeth and Margaret would follow their separate lessons with their governess.

This settling-in period was dominated by arrangements for the impending Coronation, less than three months away. In normal circumstances a year to eighteen months separates a sovereign's Accession and Coronation, but the arrangements made for Edward VIII's crowning four months hence were adhered to. Wednesday, May 12, 1937 had already been set for the – now urgent – Coronation of a new sovereign.

The Coronation of her father and mother was the first opportunity for Elizabeth to show her style for a great occasion when she was nearer the centre of events. One of the Queen's schoolgirl essays records the day. It was entitled: 'The Coronation, 12 May 1937. To Mummy and Papa. In memory of their Coronation. From Lilibet by herself.'

She wrote: 'I leapt out of bed and so did Bobo. We put on dressing-gowns and shoes and Bobo made me put on an eiderdown as it was so cold and we crouched in the window looking on to a cold misty morning.

'Every now and then we were hopping in and out of bed looking at the bands and the soldiers. At six o'clock Bobo got up and instead of getting up at my usual time I jumped out of bed by half past seven.'

While Princess Elizabeth felt grown-up enough to take everything in her stride, she worried about her seven-year-old sister. 'She is very young for a coronation, isn't she?' she said to Bobo.

Both Princesses had always dressed alike and the Coronation followed the same pattern. Their dresses were of white lace, adorned with silver bows. On their heads they wore light-weight coronets, specially fashioned by order of the King, and from their shoulders fell trains of purple velvet trimmed with ermine.

Queen Mary travelled in the Irish State Coach with Elizabeth and Margaret to the Coronation Service at Westminster Abbey. Observers of the day claim the cheers were louder for Queen Mary and the Princesses than they were for the King and Queen.

In her diary Queen Mary wrote: 'Lilibet and Margaret looked too sweet in their lace dresses and robes, especially when they put on their coronets.'

The accession of the King, at the age of 41, was not only a shock for the new monarch but it affected his daughters' lives also. 'Nothing in the Abdication cut so deep as the changed future for their children – it was hardest of all for their sake,' said Queen Elizabeth's brother, Sir David Bowes-Lyon.

In his farewell broadcast Edward VIII had said of his brother: 'He has one matchless blessing, enjoyed by so many of you and not bestowed on me – a happy home with his wife and children.'

Happy, yes, but an entirely different atmosphere was now surrounding Princess Elizabeth. The excitement of dressing up for a coronation over, Elizabeth and Margaret had to settle down to a bewildering new routine of living in a huge house, at the centre of global attention, and with parents who no longer had as much time to spare for them.

It was in this period that the bond between Elizabeth and Bobo MacDonald become so strong. She saw less of her parents, although each evening the King tried to set aside time to talk to her about monarchy, but there was a more formal atmosphere in the home.

She still went with her sister to their parents' bedrooms in the morning, but the King and Queen were often elsewhere for lunch and the bed-time romp was often abandoned or cut short because of evening engagements.

King George and Queen Elizabeth were anxious, though, that their daughters should not be cut off from the real world. Crawfie again: 'Just how difficult this is to achieve, if you live in a palace, is hard to explain. A glass curtain seems to come down between you and the other world, between the hard realities of life and those who dwell in a court.'

Children from outside the Royal circle were allowed into the Palace. A Buckingham Palace Girl Guide Company and Brownie Pack were formed. Princess Elizabeth joined the Kingfisher patrol of the Girl Guides, while Princess Margaret joined the Leprechaun Six of the Brownies. They continued Guide activities at Windsor during the Second World War, and were joined by Cockney evacuees to the Royal estate.

Elizabeth, the young teenager who was never destined for the Throne from birth, now found also that life took on a more serious aspect because she had to be trained to become a sovereign. Private lessons became more purposeful and a little of her lightheartedness disappeared as she became more involved in protocol and learning about the Affairs of State.

Life was no less difficult for her mother. As the Princesses grew older, Queen Elizabeth had to cope with the usual chores of every other mother. Helping them with their homework...making sure they behaved properly outside the home...choosing clothes and taking them to parties...and the early confusion of being teenagers. All of these duties were more difficult because the family was so much in the public eye.

Sisterly love developed in abundance in the Windsor household during these changing years as well. The playwright and popular visitor to the children, Sir James Barrie, noted: 'Princess Elizabeth's pride in her little sister whenever the Princess Margaret won a game... It was like the pride of a mother, though it began, to my eyes, when both were little more than babes.'

Elder sister kept a close watch on Margaret, though. 'If you do see someone with a funny hat, Margaret, you must *not* point at it and laugh,' she warned before a party in the grounds of Buckingham Palace.

The Heir to the Throne, described by the *Daily Telegraph* as 'Everybody's Daughter', had a forbidding educational curriculum. Languages, history, economics and deportment were just a few subjects. French, German and Latin were essential for anyone who had to understand the workings of British law and constitution.

The King and Queen helped her in her languages by speaking to her at 'French lunches' – gatherings at table where not one word of English was uttered – vital for someone who would one day be the ruler of French-speaking Quebec. It was also useful as the main second language of international communication, as Elizabeth still finds today.

As she got older, she received special tutoring in constitutional history from Sir Henry Marten, the Vice-Provost of Eton College. She also took a much greater role in official Court life, which her own children never did until their late teens.

During pre-war public appearances, when aged twelve for example, she took the salute at a march-past of scouts, and greeted President Lebrun of France...in fluent French!

In the closing years of the 1930s, however, the threat of another war was constantly in the background. At the beginning of August 1939, the Royal Family had gone on its annual Highland holiday in Balmoral. The declining political situation had already caused a delay in their departure. Princess Margaret asked indignantly, 'Who *is* this Hitler, spoiling everything?'

On September 3, Britain declared war on Germany. King George and Queen Elizabeth hastened back to London, leaving Elizabeth and Margaret in what they hoped would be peaceful Scotland.

As horrific as it was and as great as was the suffering of the British people during the Second World War, it resulted not just in victory but also gave a tremendous boost to the reputation of the Monarchy. After the Windsor debacle, Royalty needed help, and it was during those dark six years from 1939 to 1945 that the people's loyalty to the Crown was re-established. A loyalty that Elizabeth benefits from in her reign.

By the time the war broke out, most parents with money or influence were getting their children out of the cities or even out of the country altogether – to America, Canada and Australia. King George and Queen Elizabeth decided to set an example to the rest of Britain by staying as a family at home in the United Kingdom.

With his stammer and nervous air, George did not come across as a natural 'warrior king'. But he was a brave man and, as a sovereign, completely dedicated. The King himself was fully prepared to lead a resistance movement if England had been invaded.

The first Christmas of the war was spent at Sandringham, despite its proximity to one of the stretches of the Norfolk coast thought most likely to be invaded.

Elizabeth heard King George VI give a stirring message to the Empire in the traditional world-wide broadcast. After calling for a girding of the loins and recognition of the dangers facing his people, he ended with a poem that stayed for ever in the memory of the Princess.

Called *'The Gate of the Year'*, it was written by Marie Louise Haskins, a lecturer at the London School of Economics.

I said to the man who stood at the Gate of the year,
'Give me a light so that I may tread safely into the unknown,'
And he replied, 'Go out into the darkness,
And put your hand into the Hand of God.
That shall be to you better than light,
And safer than a known way.'

TEENAGE YEARS

ELIZABETH AND MARGARET stayed at Sandringham until February 1940, when they moved to Windsor Castle. It was beneath the flight path of German aircraft following the Thames to London and, in time, the Princesses could identify the bombers by the sound of their engines.

The Castle's hundreds of windows were protected, as far as possible, by stuck-on mesh, overlaid with wire-netting, and at night were lost behind thick black-out curtaining.

Against the technology of blitzkreig, the Castle was no longer the impenetrable fortress it had once been, but it still had greater facilities for the Princesses' safety than Royal Lodge, where pink walls were now hidden beneath murky camouflage.

The Castle on the banks of the Thames would become the Princesses' wartime home. If there had been a Nazi landing, a refuge had been devised in strictest secrecy. A bodyguard chosen from the Brigade of Guards and the Household Cavalry was charged with their care. Four houses in different areas were stocked with all the requirements for an emergency, and armoured cars, specially marked to ensure priority, stood by to speed them into hiding and – hopefully – safety.

George and Elizabeth slept at Windsor during the bombing raids but were always back at Buckingham Palace by daylight. Their London home was bombed twice... once on the night of September 10, 1940 and again two days later during a daring daylight raid.

They had a narrow escape during the second attack when two bombs exploded in the Palace quadrangle below the windows of a room they were both occupying at the time. When this happened Elizabeth almost succeeded to the Throne sooner than anyone expected!

A German bomber flew straight up the Mall and dropped two sticks of six bombs each on Buckingham Palace.

The King and Queen had been working together in their room when, as he wrote afterwards; 'All of a sudden we heard an aircraft making a zooming noise above us. Saw two bombs falling past the opposite side of the Palace and then heard two resounding crashes as the bombs fell in the quadrangle about thirty yards away. We looked at each other and then we were out in the passage as fast as we could get there... We all wondered why we weren't dead...'

The huge Queen Victoria Memorial shielded them from the blast. Otherwise they might have been killed.

A basement room in Buckingham Palace was converted into an air-raid shelter, although the style wasn't quite that of most back-garden dug-outs! It was furnished with Regency chairs and a settee, and the reading matter, replaced regularly by servants, was mainly hunting-shooting-and-fishing or society magazines, such as *Country Life* and *Sphere*.

Bombs fell six times on Royal homes during the war, including 145 Piccadilly. It was completely destroyed. When invasion seemed imminent in the late summer of 1940, there was increased pressure from the Government, led by Winston Churchill, for Elizabeth and her sister to be sent to Canada, both for safety and to protect the Royal line. The Queen would not have it, explaining: 'The children cannot go without me, and I cannot possibly leave the King.' She took up revolver training, nevertheless.

The family, at the Royal mother's insistence, shared where possible the deprivation of the rest of Britain. They had no further clothes other than the normal rationing allowance, making do with what they had collected before the war...frequently patched up for six years.

Heating in the Palace was cut to a minimum. Extra warm woollies had to do, while just a tiny electric fire would heat bedrooms. To save fuel again, there was a line painted five inches above the plug-holes in baths to mark the emergency hot water mark.

Meals were the same as everyone else getting by on rationing. But of course certain standards had to be maintained. So the mainly meatless sausages and powdered eggs were still served up on gold and silver dishes!

Among the foreign Royals who fled to Britain after the Nazi invasion of Northern Europe and stayed with Elizabeth's family was Queen Wilhelmina of the Netherlands. She brought with her the future Queen Juliana and grand-daughters Beatrix and Irene. A friendship was struck between the British Queen to-be and the Dutch monarchy that is still strong forty-five years afterwards.

Although sheltered for the most part from the daily stresses of the war, there were many reminders of the struggle beyond the Palace walls. The Princesses met evacuee children from the Glasgow slums when they were accommodated on the Royal estate at Balmoral.

When the menacing voice of William Joyce, better known as 'Lord Haw-Haw', Hitler's anti-British propaganda 'star', was heard on the radio, Lilibet and Margaret would throw books, cushions and any other handy missiles at the set.

Elizabeth made her first broadcast herself at the age of fourteen when, at her own request, she spoke to the children of the Empire. In her five-minute broadcast, transmitted by the BBC on October 13, 1940 during *Children's Hour*, the Princess told her audience, 'I can truthfully say to you that we children at home are full of cheerfulness and courage. We are trying to do all we can to help our gallant sailors, soldiers and airmen, and we are trying, too, to bear our own share of the danger and sadness of war. We know, every one of us, that in the end all will be well.'

She ended with: 'My sister is by my side, and we are both going to say goodnight to you. Come on, Margaret.'

Then the two of them, speaking in unison, finished the broadcast with the words... 'Good night and good luck to you all.' All this when the possibility of Britain being conquered was highly likely. Old Queen Mary is said to have broken into tears as she listened.

During the first Christmas at Windsor, in December 1940, the Princesses and local evacuees acted a nativity play, which was so successful that their ambitions rose to a full length pantomime.

With the help of a master and pupils from the Royal School at Windsor Great Park, they performed Cinderella. Their stage was the one erected by Queen Victoria in the Waterloo Room for earlier family theatricals.

The King was thrilled by their confidence: 'I don't know how they do it,' he said. 'We were always so terribly shy and self-conscious as children. These two don't seem to care.'

The two sisters' love of theatricals was given further outlet on subsequent Christmases with performances of *The Sleeping Beauty* in 1942, *Aladdin* – in which the princesses' young cousins, the Duke of Kent and Princess Alexandra were also cast – in 1943, and *Old Mother Red Riding Boots* in 1944.

A further outlet for Royal talents was the Royal Windsor Society, which included among its enthusiasts young Guards officers and boys from Eton public school.

As Elizabeth got older, she was introduced into the company of selected teenage boys and young men of the 'right background.' There was the practice, for example, of inviting two officers of the Guards to join herself and Margaret for lunch every day at Windsor.

As she approached womanhood and her pre-destined role, Elizabeth would join her father and go through the famous 'red boxes' containing State papers, which are part of the daily life of a British sovereign. George would confide in her as in an equal, and as she grew older he took the greatest trouble to initiate her into her future role. When she was sixteen he made her Colonel-in-Chief of the Grenadier Guards. She took her duties so earnestly, though, that after one inspection he passed the word to her that 'the first requisite of a really good officer is to be able to temper justice with mercy.'

There were suggestions from some Royal and political circles that when Elizabeth reached eighteen that she should be given the traditional title of an Heir to the Throne, Princess of Wales.

The King turned it down. He told his mother, 'How could I create Lilibet the Princess of Wales when it is the recognised title of the wife of the Prince of Wales? Her own name is so nice and what name would she be called by when she marries I want to know?'

When she was eighteen, however, and old enough, Elizabeth joined the Army, wearing khaki as an officer in the Auxiliary Territorial Service, the predecessor of today's Women's Royal Army Corps.

Few people who meet the Queen when she is in silken and bejewelled finery realise that those well-manicured hands have suffered their fair share of broken nails, cuts and oily bruises while servicing lorries. The Sovereign can count among her many talents that of a trained motor mechanic, a skill she acquired during her Army days.

The King and Queen felt it would be very useful for her to learn driving and maintenance with the ATS. It would also give her an insight into how other girls lived. She did not go through the ranks, though, and eleven other girls were carefully chosen to accompany her on the brief course.

She was commissioned as a Second Subaltern and took immense pride in the fact that she was now serving the war effort like other girls of her age. Apart from returning to Windsor to sleep, she kept strictly to the routine, taking her turn with others as duty officer, doing inspections, and working hard on vehicle maintenance.

Number 230873 Second Subaltern The Princess Elizabeth learned how to strip and service an engine, and became proficient in vehicle maintenance, although she was never to see active service because the war in Europe ended three weeks after her training course ended.

On V.E. (Victory-in-Europe) Day crowds flocked to Buckingham Palace as the King and Queen with the Princesses and Winston Churchill stepped on to the Palace balcony. 'We went out eight times altogether during the afternoon and evening,' noted the King in his diary. 'We were given a great reception.'

After many balcony appearances the King suggested that Elizabeth and Margaret should slip out with an escort of young officers to join the excited crowds below. He wanted them to experience at street level the drama of the occasion. He felt the war had robbed them of many youthful pleasures: 'Poor darlings,' he also wrote that night, 'they have never had any fun yet.'

They slipped unobtrusively through the Palace gates to join in the fun. A policeman's helmet was playfully knocked off by their uncle, David Bowes-Lyon, who offered a tongue-in-cheek apology as the Princesses 'ran off in case they were caught.'

Elizabeth sent a message into the Palace saying they were outside and would Their Majesties oblige just once more? When the doors of the balcony were opened yet again the two Princesses joined in the cheering with the crowds.

The future head of the British Army was wearing her ATS uniform but she had taken off her cap. A more senior officer in the Guards passing by noticed this, reprimanded her and ordered her to be 'properly dressed.' He did not then know who she was, and whoever *he was* has kept secret his identity to this day.

The Royal Family emerged from the war years with its reputation revitalised to become the institution that is now so respected and loved. Churchill was able to write to George after victory was won: 'This war has drawn the Throne and the People more closely together than was ever before recorded, and Your Majesties are more beloved by all classes and conditions than any of the princes of the past.'

FALLING IN LOVE

WHEN THE Royal Family looked around them they found that inside the Palace carpets were threadbare and patched, while outside too, London and the rest of Britain carried the scars of war. After the euphoria of national celebrations, the struggle to get the country back on its feet had begun.

The soldiers, sailors and airmen returned. Among the sailors was Lieutenant Prince Philip of Greece. His arrival had a remarkable effect on Elizabeth. She had taken to playing over and over again on the gramophone the 'Oklahoma' hit, *'People will say we're in love...'*

On a desk in her room for more than a year there had been a photograph of the fair-haired sailor prince, which was recently replaced by a new one in which the face was hidden behind a bushy beard and made him almost totally unrecognisable.

Princess Elizabeth's romance with Philip was so delightfully uncomplicated that it was almost out of a fairy tale, compared to sister Margaret's later fiery relationships.

When Princess Elizabeth showed an interest in this young Naval chap who was a protégé of his uncle, Lord Louis Mountbatten – Uncle Dickie – her mother saw the signs as long ago as the pre-war days when Philip had met her daughter at Dartmouth Naval College, in Devon.

Philip and Elizabeth had met before Dartmouth but never really noticed each other until then. They had been briefly together at the same Royal functions – the marriage of Philip's cousin, Princess Marina, to the Duke of Kent, for example, and the Coronation of Elizabeth's father. But the difference in ages was too great for them to have taken any more than a cursory interest in each other.

At the time of her father's Coronation, the future Queen was only eleven, while he was sixteen and already a young man. Lord Mountbatten, was in attendance as the King's ADC on the day of the visit to the Naval college, so it seemed natural that another Royal relative, Philip, should be appointed Captain's doggie (messenger) for the day.

There was a special service in the college chapel, which Elizabeth and Margaret would normally have attended with their parents, but because some of the college cadets had developed mumps, it was felt wiser for the girls to stay away. Instead they went along to the Captain's (Sir Frederick Hew George Dalrymple-Hamilton) house to play with the Dalrymple-Hamilton children, a slightly older boy and girl.

The slim, ash-blond Philip joined them, helping the younger children operate a toy train set, munching biscuits with them, drinking lemonade. He showed the Princesses the college swimming-pool and also played croquet with them. When the Royal Yacht set sail again, the college cadets piled into a variety of small craft to escort it out to sea.

Some followed it too far. They were signalled to turn back. All except one did so. The exception was Philip. He continued to pull at the oars of the small boat he was rowing. Elizabeth watched him through binoculars, taking a long, final glimpse at the young man she had begun to set her heart on.

She developed a teenage crush on this man who was her third cousin through their joint links created generations earlier by Queen Victoria.

Two years later Princess Elizabeth and Prince Philip had a second meeting at Buckingham Palace, and they kept up a steady correspondence during the war years, when he was serving on destroyers.

He often used to spend his leaves at Windsor Castle, and there was one pantomime when Princess Elizabeth cared very much how well she acted – for Philip was in the front row.

The Queen Mother, not being quite sure of her husband's reaction, knew what was going on and decided to allow matters to take their natural course. All she ever wanted was her daughter's happiness. When it dawned on the King that his daughter – by now seventeen – was interested in Lord Louis' nephew, he argued that Elizabeth was too young and too inexperienced to think of marriage. Just as any other father would.

He told Queen Mary in 1944: 'We both think she is too young for that now, as she has never met any young man of her own age. I like Philip. He is intelligent, has a good sense of humour and thinks about things in the right way.' Then there was the sting in the tail: 'Philip had better not think any more about it for the present.'

Despite this early fatherly opposition, mother Elizabeth thought she had better take a hand, and when the war was over, Philip was among the first guests at Balmoral and Buckingham Palace. He became a frequent visitor, encouraged by his future mother-in-law's enthusiasm.

Whenever he could get leave from his Naval duties he would be there, even though the King wanted Elizabeth to meet a wider cicle of men, and at every opportunity eligible suitors were introduced into her company. They never stood a chance. The Queen Mother, with an eye for romance, was delighted to see this.

Philip was a prince of Greece, an heir to the Greek throne – but without a drop of Greek blood in his veins. On his father's side, he came from the Danish royal house of Schleswig-Holstein-Sonderburg-Glücksburg which, in the days when monarchs ruled as well as reigned, supplied not only Denmark with its kings but exported them also to Greece, Sweden, Norway and Russia.

On his mother's side, he was descended from the Mountbattens, who were Battenbergs until they changed the family name, and could trace their lineage back through some forty-four generations to approximately 600 AD.

He also had some English blood from Queen Victoria and a sprinkling of the Russian Romanov. George I of Greece married the teenage Grand Duchess Olga of Russia. They had two daughters and five sons, one of whom was Prince Andrew, Philip's father. Andrew married Alice, the daughter of Princess Victoria of Hesse and her cousin, Prince Louis of Battenberg.

Andrew's brother, Constantine, took over the throne on the assassination of their father. Constantine was married to a sister of the German Emperor, which did not go down too well with Britain and France during the First World War.

They intervened to depose him and install his second son, Alexander, in his place. In 1920, Alexander was bitten by a pet monkey. Blood poisoning set in and he died in agony.

A plebiscite in Greece favoured recalling the exiled Constantine as king. So back they all trekked from exile in Switzerland, including Andrew and Alice, now pregnant. She gave birth to Philip on June 10, 1921, on a dining-room table in a Royal villa on the island of Corfu.

When Philip was one year old, Prince Andrew was charged with treason and sentenced to death after his regiment was ignominiously routed by the Turks in one of the frequent Balkan conflicts. Only the intervention of King George V saved his life.

Soon afterwards the leaders of a revolution in Greece kicked Andrew and his family out of the country and took away his nationality. He went into exile on board the British cruiser *Calypso*, with Philip sleeping in a padded cot made by the ship's carpenters from an old orange box.

It was now that the Mountbatten family came so strongly into Philip's life. The elder of the two Mountbatten brothers, George, successor to his father as Marquis of Milford Haven, brought his sister Alice and her young son to Britain.

His own son, David, was already a boarder at Cheam, the preparatory school for the children of upper-class parents. He sent Philip there, where he became completely Anglicised, receiving the education of a little English gentleman. Philip developed a friendship with David which was to continue into young adulthood.

Within two years his sisters were married to German princelings. Sophie, the youngest, became the bride of Prince Christopher of Hesse, later to be killed while flying with the Luftwaffe in the Second World War.

The German links with Philip increased when, in his early teens, he was sent to Salem School on the shore of Lake Constance, where Berthold of Baden, married to his sister Theodora, was headmaster.

The founder of the school, Dr. Kurt Hahn, a Jew, moved to the Highlands of Scotland and set up a new establishment at Gordonstoun in 1934. He did this to escape the attentions of Hitler and brought thirty of his boys with him, including Philip.

When Philip arrived at Salem he found that most of the teachers were members of the Nazi party and the boys were compelled to become members of the Hitler Youth movement. 'Heil Hitlers' were compulsory in the classroom. As a foreigner Philip was excused such indoctrination.

At Gordonstoun, famous for cold showers and a tough regime, Philip proved himself an outstanding member of the school. He was popular. He was a fine athlete and became a skilled sailor, learning his seamanship out on the chilly, choppy waters of the Moray Firth. He became Guardian, Gordonstoun's name for head boy.

Academically he did not fare so well, and he left school without the qualifications necessary for university or college. By this time Philip's mother and father had separated and the strain was such that he was placed in the guardianship of his uncle George, 2nd Marquess of Milford Haven. George died unexpectedly when Philip was seventeen, and so the guardianship passed to the next uncle, Lord Mountbatten; an association that was to shape Philip's future – and that of the British Monarchy.

It was Lord Mountbatten who directed his nephew to the Royal Naval College at Dartmouth even though, if the choice had been his, he would rather have joined the Royal Air Force. If he had gone to Cranwell, the R.A.F. college, it is highly unlikely that he and Elizabeth would have met in such romantic circumstances.

According to Sir John Wheeler-Bennett, the official biographer of George VI, 'This was the man with whom Princess Elizabeth had been in love from their first meeting.'

After graduating from Dartmouth just before the outbreak of the war, he went to sea as a second lieutenant. Two years later he faced his first blooding in action on board a battleship against the Italian fleet off Cape Matapan. For his courageous and cool behaviour under fire he was mentioned in despatches.

He was serving on the battleship *Valiant* and manning a searchlight in the middle of fierce shell fire. His Captain said of him: 'Thanks to his alertness and appreciation of the situation we were able to sink in five minutes two eight-inch gun Italian cruisers.'

Prince Philip was too busy with his war service to think too seriously about the future, but in 1944, when Elizabeth was eighteen, he asked his cousin, King George of Greece, to find out how a match between them would be viewed. 'We both think she is too young for that now,' replied George VI, 'as she has never met any young men of her own age... Philip had better not think any more about it for the present.' They were the same stinging words used to Queen Mary a year earlier.

But the war over, he became a more frequent visitor to the Palace and Elizabeth. A prince of Royal birth he might be, but he had a number of black marks against him. His religion was wrong: he was Greek Orthodox. He had no money. He was not British. His German ancestry was an embarrassment so soon after the war.

The King was firm. 'You must be patient and wait a while', he told his elder daughter when she was twenty. Philip was given a shore job by the

Navy and had more time for Elizabeth. The King played his last card when he began throwing receptions at the Palace so that Elizabeth could meet a wide range of young men. In any event he did not relish the prospect of losing his daughter so soon after he was, at last, able to spend more time with her...time which the early years of kingship and the war had denied him.

Elizabeth was independent of mind and strong of will, though – and in love. Philip formally proposed to her in the summer of 1946. She first accepted him and only then went off to tell her parents. The King did not raise any more objections but insisted on delaying any announcement.

Philip and Elizabeth reluctantly agreed to her parent's insistence on delay, at least until her twenty-first birthday the following year. Philip was persuaded meanwhile to shed his awkward birthright and become plain Lieutenant Philip Mountbatten.

Philip and Elizabeth were parted when the two Princesses went with their parents on a tour of South Africa in 1947. The Queen Mother noticed that her elder daughter was quiet and subdued when she was told about the African trip.

The Royal Family sailed in the Navy's newest battleship, *Vanguard*, which Princess Elizabeth had launched two years previously. They left Portsmouth on January 31 on what was to be the last overseas tour of George VI's reign. Their departure coincided with the worst British winter within living memory. Ice, snow, gales and fog paralysed the country. Within four days, two million people had been thrown out of work by a chronic coal shortage. Food ships were held up in the docks and supply trains halted by snowfalls.

As the Royal party sailed into the sun, young Elizabeth wrote in her diary, 'While we are scorching, we feel rather guilty at being right away from it all.' When the *Vanguard* arrived at Cape Town, a reporter for the African channel on local radio is reputed to have described the Royal quartet as 'The King and the Queen and the fruit of their loins, Elizabeth and Margaret.'

King George and his family travelled ten thousand miles by car or train in two months – an average of two hundred miles for every day of the tour. There was a succession of receptions, inspections, official dinners, parties – rest days were few and far between. It was a tough schedule of functions for Elizabeth and Margaret: meetings with tribes and their chiefs, inspections of military units, visits to national shrines and natural beauty spots. On free days, they went riding and swimming. They would cool down in pleasant, picturesque lakes.

It was noticed by members of the entourage that Elizabeth seemed to be unusually quiet and moody at times. This was put down to the forbidden subject – Philip back home. The delicate subject of her relationship with Philip was raised at a barbecue reception in Orange Free State. A member of the Provincial Council approached Elizabeth and asked her whether it was true that she would soon announce her engagement. She smiled and said nothing.

When driving through the Reef towns in an open Daimler limousine one day, a huge Zulu burst from the crowd and rushed towards the slow-moving car, shouting with apparent ferocity. His fingers clutched the car and he hung on with something shining in his free hand while the Queen beat him off with her parasol until it broke in two.

The police knocked him down, thinking they were dealing with a potential assassin. In fact he was clutching a ten-shilling note loyally intended as a birthday gift for Princess Elizabeth.

She had celebrated her twenty-first birthday with that famous broadcast to the Commonwealth. She said her message was *'Very simple...I declare before you all that my whole life, whether it be long or short, shall be devoted to your service and the service of our great Imperial Commonwealth to which we all belong.'*

The separation in South Africa did not kill the romance, and when the Royal Family returned to Britain, George, at his wife's behest, had to accept that Philip and Elizabeth were deeply in love.

After the family reached London in May 1947, the King spent two months thinking about Philip as a prospective son-in-law. Thorough inquiries were made into his background. Then, early in July, Elizabeth drew Margaret to one side and brought her left hand forward from behind her back where she had kept it hidden. Margaret cried out when she saw the diamond engagement ring.

The official Court Circular of Wednesday, July 9, 1947 announced: *'It is with great pleasure that the King and Queen announce the betrothal of their dearly beloved daughter, the Princess Elizabeth, to Lieutenant Philip Mountbatten, RN, son of the late Prince Andrew, to which union the King has gladly given his consent.'*

PRINCESS ELIZABETH was twenty-one, her fiancé twenty-six. The news that the King had told Elizabeth that she could marry her sailor brought the first post-war cheer to a glum world in 1947.

After announcing the engagement, King George VI mused: 'He's the right man for the job, but I wonder if he knows what he's taking on. One day Lilibet will be Queen and he will be Consort. And that's much harder than being a king.' The King had just under five years to live – Philip's role in the Monarchy, with all its problems, was much nearer than anyone imagined.

The engagement came not only as gloomy Britain was just recovering from a terrible winter, but also at a time when the harsh realities of recovering from a war that had virtually bankrupted the nation had to be faced up to. In addition, Burma had left the British Empire, and India – for long 'the jewel in the British Crown' – was about to become independent.

Relations between Russia and the West were also crumbling fast – the Cold War was about to begin. Little wonder, then, that Winston Churchill greeted the Royal love match with the comment: 'A flash of colour on the hard road we have to travel.'

Elizabeth and Philip's first public appearance together was at a garden party in the grounds of Buckingham Palace. He wore his Naval uniform, looking decidedly shabby after its long wartime use.

On July 15, they went north to Holyrood House, the official home in Edinburgh of the Royal Family, to a tremendous welcome from the citizens of the Scottish capital. King George said that he and the Queen were specially touched during the visit by the friendliness of the citizens and were 'delighted to observe the spontaneous affection towards Princess Elizabeth in connection with her engagement.'

There was a reluctance in Government circles to agree to a huge and expensive wedding in a period when there were hundreds of thousands homeless and the State coffers were almost empty. A newspaper carried out an opinion poll among its readers, asking: 'Should the Princess's wedding day be selected as the first post-war occasion to restore to Britain the traditional gaiety of a gala public event?' More than eighty-six per cent answered 'Yes'.

A date was set for the Royal Wedding – Thursday, November 20, 1947. It would be the first wedding in English history of an Heiress Presumptive who would one day become Queen.

Bearing in mind that the Government was against a 'big splash', King George VI decided that there should be no lavish display. He also decided that he would pay all the wedding expenses from his own Privy Purse, apart from street decorations in Whitehall and the Mall. He would also cover the expenses of the newly-weds for two years after the wedding.

Thought had been given to a private, quiet wedding in St. George's Chapel at Windsor, but more extravagant heads among the Royal advisers decided to be daring and choose Westminster Abbey – the traditional venue for the crowning and marrying of monarchs.

A place to live had to be found for the happy couple. George decided to give them Clarence House, the mansion on the left side of The Mall from Buckingham Palace, which had not been used as a Royal residence for five years. It had suffered badly from bombing during the war and needed expensive repairs.

Until their new home was ready, it was decided that Elizabeth and Philip would move into Buckingham Palace and live with the bride's family. As they would have six hundred rooms to choose from, the couple were unlikely to get in the way of the 'in-laws'...

George also handed over the keys to Sunninghill Park, a large house near Windsor, for use as a weekend retreat. Unfortunately it caught fire two weeks later and was gutted. For the Royal bride-to-be the fire was a shattering blow. She and Philip had looked forward to using Sunninghill, with its marble staircases and a lake in secluded grounds, as their own private hideaway.

Presents began to arrive from all parts of the globe. Gifts of every imaginable kind – enormously expensive or kind gestures from humble folk. A team of Genadier Guardsmen worked full-time unpacking them.

The King and his wife gave their daughter a Nineteenth Century necklace of oblong sapphires set in diamonds, separated by diamond collets, and a matching pair of sapphire drop earrings surrounded by diamonds. In the summer of 1952 the necklace was shortened; a pendant was added in 1959.

Another wedding present from her parents was a pair of diamond chandelier earrings with three drops which contained every known modern cut. It was four years, however, before these beautiful earrings were worn. Although she had begun to wear ear-clips at the age of eighteen, she did not have her ears pierced until the eve of her visit to Canada in 1951.

Among the humbler offerings were a home-made plastic brooch from a schoolgirl, kettleholders knitted by old-age pensioners, a bed of rhododendrons, and a table mat spun by the Indian leader, Mahatma Gandhi himself.

When this arrived there was considerable surprise at the Palace. Then the story of the Gandhi table mat became clear.

When Gandhi heard about the engagement he summoned the last Viceroy of India, Lord Mountbatten, to pass on his congratulations. He said, though, that he could give no wedding present since he had no possessions. 'You can spin,' replied Mountbatten, 'and have it made into something.' So Gandhi's spinning wheel made the yarn and a table mat was crocheted to his own design. All told, 3007 presents were received. They were later shown to the public, who queued in their thousands to see them in St. James's Palace.

Hard days there may have been but, according to the writings of Lady Airlie, Queen Mary's lady-in-waiting, there was 'a week of gaiety such as the court had not seen for years. There were parties at St. James's Palace to view the wedding presents, a Royal dinner party for all the foreign royalties, and an evening party at Buckingham Palace which seemed, after the years of austerity, like a scene out of a fairy tale.'

More than most bridegrooms, Philip found himself forced to take a back seat in the arrangements for his own wedding. With a future queen as a bride, even her own mother did not have much of a say. The wedding became a national event. Other forces moved in and took over.

The hardest blow of all for Philip to bear during all the wedding preparations was that his sisters' names were not included on the invitation list. Invitations could go to his mother and other relatives, even to old friends, but not to his sisters.

By marrying Germans they had become German nationals, and with the Second World War still fresh in British minds, anyone German, however closely related, could not be invited. The best Philip could do was arrange an extra set of wedding photographs to be printed for his sisters. His cousin, Princess Marina, obligingly flew out to Germany with them shortly after the wedding.

It was also unthinkable to King George VI that his elder daughter, the future Queen, should emerge from the Abbey as Princess Mrs. Lieutenant Mountbatten.

So on the eve of the wedding the King invited Philip to give up his Greek title as a prince and honoured him with British titles. He was created a Royal Highness, Baron Greenwich, Earl of Merioneth and Duke of Edinburgh. 'It is a great deal to give a man all at once, but I know Philip understands his new responsibilities on his marriage to Lilibet,' said George.

He reverted to 'Prince' again ten years later when the, by now, Queen Elizabeth declared he was a 'Prince of the United Kingdom'.

The day of the wedding was grey but mild. The Mall was lined with thirty-two tall poles, hung with yellow and white banners bearing 'E' in gold and red medallions. The crowd was enormous. Nothing like it had been seen in London since the Coronation ten years previously...a happy, good-tempered crowd determined to enjoy a brief escape from austerity. Flags and streamers flowered from every hand.

The bride and her father travelled to Westminster Abbey in the Irish State Coach, drawn by four greys and escorted by a sovereign's escort of the Royal Household Cavalry, their polished cuirasses flashing. The Guard of Honour at the West door of the Abbey was formed from the Royal Navy and the three regiments with which the bride was connected – the Grenadier Guards, of which she was Colonel-in-Chief, the 16th/5th Lancers, and the Argyll and Sutherland Highlanders, of which she was Colonel-in-Chief.

Among one of the largest ever gatherings of royalty were the Kings and Queens of Norway, Denmark, the Hellenes, Rumania, Yugoslavia, Spain and Iraq. Crown princes and princesses came from the Netherlands, Belgium, Sweden and Luxembourg.

Wartime clothes rationing was still in force, so a hundred clothing coupons were needed to make the Princess's gown. Twenty-five each were allotted to her bridesmaids.

She wore, on this day of pageantry and history, a dress of ivory satin, woven in Scotland, with fitted bodice, long, tight sleeves, and a full skirt. It was richly embroidered with pearls in a design of roses, stars and ears of wheat; the gossamer fifteen-foot long train was appliqué with the same design in white satin. The whole creation, described by one observer as 'sheer poetry', was designed by Royal couturier, Norman Hartnell.

Elizabeth carried a bouquet of white orchids, which had caused a last-minute flurry when it had been temporarily mislaid. On her head was her mother's sunray diamond tiara, and, as a Royal Bride, her veil was flung back.

The eight bridesmaids, mainly cousins, led by Princess Margaret, wore what Vogue described as 'ethereal ivory silk tulle gowns with pearl-spotted fichu and billowing flower-appliqué skirts.' Behind them in the procession down the aisle of the Abbey came Princess Elizabeth's household, her ladies-in-waiting in draped dresses of cyclamen and sea-green crêpe.

Philip was happy to wear a new standard issue Naval uniform. He did sport, however, a smart Naval sword decorated with golden tassels. He had chosen as his best man David, the Marquess of Milford Haven, his closest friend.

George VI told his daughter later that when he escorted her to the altar: 'I was so proud of you and thrilled at having you so close to me on our long walk in Westminster Abbey, but when I handed your hand to the Archbishop I felt that I had lost something very precious. You were so calm and composed during the service and said your words with such conviction.'

There had been a family discussion a week earlier of the marriage vows. Elizabeth had decided that she did not mind in the least promising to 'obey' her husband. Queen presumptive or not, she wanted a traditional marriage like any other bride.

The Archbishop of York said in his address that in essence the ceremony was 'exactly the same as it would be for any cottager who might be married this afternoon in some small country church in a remote village in the dales.'

As Elizabeth and Philip drove back to Buckingham Palace for the first time as man and wife, it is said that the bride's eyes were shining with a hint of tears. 'Good old Philip!' she heard the crowds shouting. Philip was still nervous and not yet accustomed to public adulation.

Back at the Palace there was a wedding breakfast for 150 guests in the first-floor ballroom. It was remarkably brief – twenty minutes – and consisted of a three-course meal (*filet de sole Mountbatten, perdreau en casserole* – meat with new potatoes and beans – *and bombe glacée Princess Elizabeth*). The speeches were kept to the minimum.

While the family and guests ate their food at an indigestive pace, the King's Pipe-Major, at the head of four pipes from Balmoral, marched up and down the room playing traditional Scottish airs. The four-tier wedding cake was cut with Philip's sword before the couple were toasted in champagne.

For their honeymoon the newly-weds had been offered Broadlands, the vast and château-like stately home in Hampshire belonging to Lord Mountbatten. They spent only a few days there because sightseers persisted in invading their privacy. To get away from the curious they dashed up to another Royal home at Birkhall, near Balmoral.

Princess Elizabeth sent a letter from there to her parents thanking them for all they had done. Her father's reply included this poignant paragraph: 'Your leaving us has left a great blank in our lives, but do remember that your old home is still yours and do come back to it as much and as often as possible. I can see that you are sublimely happy with Philip, which is right, but don't forget us. This is the wish of your ever-loving and devoted Papa.'

He also wrote: 'Our family, us four, the "Royal Family", must remain together, with additions, of course, at suitable moments!! I have watched you grow up all these years with pride under the skilful direction of Mummy, who, as you know, is the most marvellous person in the world in my eyes, and I can, I know, always count on you, and now Philip, to help us in our work.'

Marrying Princess Elizabeth brought Philip a stable family life for the first time. Until then he had been virtually a nomad, living with relations in Europe; a solitary Naval officer who had never really known a permanent anchorage. Even now a marital home of his own, with Elizabeth, had to be put off. After the interrupted honeymoon, they moved into the Palace where they lived for another eighteen months before Clarence House was ready for them.

But they were ready for parenthood...and so Prince Charles came into the world one gloomy Sunday evening a year after their marriage.

They knew nothing of the darkening clouds ahead. In the last few weeks of her pregnancy, but unknown to Elizabeth, her father – a heavy smoker – began to develop symptoms of the cancer that was to lead to his death. King George consulted his doctor about the pain in October 1948. Specialists were called in. Far from dispelling anxiety, they took a much more serious view than had been anticipated. It was King George who gave the orders that the bad news should be kept from Elizabeth until after the baby was born.

Elizabeth hoped that her first child would arrive on her first wedding anniversary, but in fact it was six days earlier, on November 14, 1948, that a policeman announced to the waiting crowd: 'IT'S A BOY!' This time there was no embarrassed Home Secretary waiting to confirm the Royal birth. George VI had killed off this outdated and unnecessary tradition.

The Princess had insisted on having her baby at home in her own room, but in fact the Buhl Room on the first floor of the Palace was made ready as a surgery. Two days earlier the King had undergone investigative surgery, and, as his first grandchild came into the world, he was lying in pain in another room not far away. The first bulletin on his health was not made public until nine days later.

Instead of pacing up and down in the classic style of an expectant father, Prince Philip sweated away the hours before the birth with hectic games of squash, and swimming in the Palace pool. When the news came he bounded up the stairs three at a time and was by the Princess's bedside with a bouquet of carnations and roses as she came round from the anaesthetic.

Outside the Palace the birth brought crowds surging to swell the numbers who had been waiting there all day. In Trafalgar Square the fountains ran blue for a boy and 4,000 telegrams of congratulation reached Elizabeth and Philip the same night. By midnight the police had to disperse the noisy but happy crowd so that mother and baby could get some sleep. The ailing George VI also could not rest because of the enthusiasm outside.

Next day bells, cannon and beacons welcomed the new Prince. The celebrations went on and on and by evening another crowd had gathered, this time to sing lullabies outside Buckingham Palace. Elizabeth wrote to a friend: 'Don't you think he is quite adorable? I still can't believe he is really mine, but perhaps that happens to new parents. Anyway, this particular boy's parents couldn't be more proud of him. It's wonderful to think, isn't it, that his arrival could give a bit of happiness to so many people, beside ourselves, at this time?'

As they proudly showed off their first-born Elizabeth and Philip were giving some thought to names. After the death of Albert, Prince Consort, Queen Victoria ruled that all male descendants should be named after her beloved husband. But they ignored orders from the past, from a previous century's Throne, and decided to call him Charles Philip Arthur George. Within a few years, and while still a toddler, he was also to become Duke of Cornwall, Duke of Rothesay, Earl of Carrick and Baron of Renfrew, Lord of the Isles and Great Steward of Scotland.

Charles was the first male in direct succession for more than eighty years. When, twenty years later, he was given the traditional title of the Heir, Prince of Wales, he would continue the ancestral line of a pageant of Royalty that included Edward, the classical armour-clad Black Prince of the Fourteenth Century – who used to feature in so may Hollywood epics starring either Robert Taylor or Tony Curtis – the marriage-prone Henry VIII, and the man who gave his name to both a style of living and an era, Queen Victoria's son, Edward VII.

Discovery of his fate, however, did not come to Charles until he was about eight years old. He now remembers: 'I didn't suddenly wake up in my pram one day and say 'Yippee'. I think it just dawns on you slowly that people are interested in you and you slowly get the idea that you have a certain duty and responsibility. I think it's better that way, rather than someone suddenly telling you.'

Charles' christening took place in the blue-columned Music Room overlooking the gardens at Buckingham Palace. The Chapel had been bombed during the war. The gold lily font, made for the christening of the Princess Royal one hundred and eight years earlier and used to baptise the Royal Mum when she was born, was pressed into service again. It was brought from Windsor and again filled with water from the River Jordan. Among the family circle at the service were four surviving grand-daughters of Queen Victoria, who had themselves worn the same lace christening robe. The ceremony was performed by the Archbishop of Canterbury, Dr. Fisher.

For the first few months of her motherhood, Elizabeth breast-fed her baby, but then, as she had to resume a normal public life, she handed over Charles into the care of two Scottish nurses, Miss Helen Lightbody and Miss Mabel Anderson. A few months later Elizabeth and Philip's first home was ready. So they moved into Clarence House, where Charles was settled in a pale blue nursery. The private gardens at the back of the house led on to St. James's Park and here the baby, trailed discreetly by detectives, was often taken for an airing in an old pram that had been used years earlier for Elizabeth and Margaret.

When not on Royal duties Elizabeth threw herself wholeheartedly into the joys of motherhood. Philip meanwhile resumed his Naval career. Both expected the 50-year-old King to be on the Throne for at least another ten years. They were unaware of how seriously ill he had been, so that seemed to be their future for many years ahead.

Philip was posted to Malta as second-in-command of a destroyer, *HMS Chequers*. He was soon joined by Elizabeth to share the life of a Naval officer.

It was during the days when the British Mediterranean fleet filled Valetta Harbour, and Philip was one of hundreds of young officers belonging to a force that continued to prove that Britannia ruled the waves. He might be the husband of the future Queen, but he was also a Naval officer devoted to his career. The possibility of standing on the left-hand-side of a sovereign still seemed remote.

Like all budding Nelsons or Drakes, he had to take examinations to further his chances of promotion. While Elizabeth was with him in Malta he failed a course in anti-submarine warfare by a narrow margin. It was suggested that because the marks were so marginal he should be allowed through. When Philip heard this suggestion, he indignantly refused such an easy option and insisted on taking the examination again – this time he passed with flying colours.

Life in Malta is said to have been the closest Elizabeth ever came to a normal everyday existence, free of official duties. Sadly, it was also to be the last time. Lord Mountbatten was commanding a squadron in the Med and he allowed the couple to live in his house, the Villa Guardamangia, overlooking the harbour. From there they would go swimming, sunbathing, dancing, on picnics, for outings to beaches all round the island, and haggle in markets. There were also dinner parties with other young married couples.

Within a few months of settling down to this marvellous, hectic and 'free' life, Elizabeth was pregnant again. She flew back to Clarence House for the birth. Princess Anne Elizabeth Alice Louise was born there on August 15, 1950, a few days after Philip had dashed back from sea duties to be with his wife. The only daughter in the family was christened, like her elder brother, in the Palace Music Room.

A young mother of two adorable children; a husband with whom she enjoyed sharing what was shaping up as a successful career; a home of her own and a loving family 'just down the road' at the Palace...life, at least, on the surface, was blissfully happy for Elizabeth. In the background, alas, was the knowledge that these idyllic years were numbered.

For by now everyone in the family, and close advisers at Court, realised how seriously ill George VI had become. He spent his last years enjoying the company of his grandchildren, who would stay with him and the Queen in Buckingham Palace and at Sandringham while Elizabeth was visiting Philip in Malta.

He wrote to his eldest daughter on one occasion: 'Charles is too sweet, stumping around the room. We shall love having him at Sandringham. He is the fifth generation to live there and I hope he will get to like the place.' The King spent most of 1950 resting and trying to fight the malignant cancer in his lungs. He had to cancel public engagements and, where possible, Princess Elizabeth would carry out duties on his behalf.

By 1951 he was clearly a very sick man and in June his doctors diagnosed a 'catarrhal inflammation of the right lung'. In September, after the King's chest had been X-rayed and specimens of tissue had been taken, it was clear that he had to have a lung removed. He appeared to recover from the operation, though he was much thinner, looked even older, and had difficulty with his voice.

In October it was announced that, owing to the King's illness, he and the Queen would not be able to go on their planned tour of East Africa, Australia and New Zealand in 1952 and that Princess Elizabeth and Philip would go in their place. But by November the King was well enough to be photographed with Prince Charles on this third birthday. Early in December he introduced Princess Elizabeth and the Duke of Edinburgh as members of the Privy Council, his closest group of advisers.

During the tour of Canada and the United States, Elizabeth carried with her a sealed envelope to be opened in the event of her father's death. It contained her Accession Documents, giving her immediate powers of Sovereignty.

A bad cough forced George to undergo a second bronchoscopy just before Christmas, when his annual broadcast to Britain and the Commonwealth revealed the struggle he was having with his voice. He underwent another thorough examination on January 29, 1952 and his doctors said they were pleased with his progress. The next evening, the entire family went to see the musical, *South Pacific,* at Drury Lane Theatre as a celebration of the King's recovery and as a farewell to Princess Elizabeth and the Duke of Edinburgh before they left next day for their five-month foreign tour.

The following morning, 56-year-old George VI stood hatless on the tarmac of Heathrow Airport to bid farewell to his daughter and son-in-law. His gaunt appearance shook those watching. He appeared like a man who truly knew he was facing death; that he knew the wave he gave to his beloved Lilibet would be his last. And so it turned out.

February 6, 1952 was a day when Prince Philip and Elizabeth were resting in the Aberdare game reserve in Kenya after an exhausting first few days of their East African tour. The Royal Party was staying in a hut built in the branches of a giant fig tree. It overlooked a watering hole where animals came in the middle of the night. Elizabeth had stayed up until dawn watching elephant, rhinoceros and water-buck through binoculars.

By 10.45 a.m. London time – 1.45 p.m. in Kenya – it had been announced that King George VI had died in his sleep during the night at Sandringham. He was discovered by his assistant valet, James Macdonald when he went into the King's room at 7.30 to wake him up.

News of the tragedy reached court officials in Kenya via news agencies. They waited to confirm the messages with Buckingham Palace before letting Elizabeth know what had happened.

By now the Royal Party had returned from Treetops to a nearby hunting-lodge at Sagana.

Prince Philip's private secretary, Michael Parker, put calls through to Nairobi and London seeking information. Meanwhile, the wire services' news was being passed around among the Royal servants.

Bobo MacDonald and the Prince's valet, John Dean, were among the first to know that Elizabeth had become Queen. They were sitting on a doorstep cleaning shoes when the Princess' detective told them. The two servants continued cleaning their mistress and master's shoes. They could not think of anything else to do.

Elizabeth came out to talk to them as they sat there. She was keen to go for a ride before flying out with Philip that afternoon to resume the tour in Mombasa, and asked Bobo if she would make the necessary arrangements.

Bobo and Dean looked at each other, not knowing what to do or to say. They decided to behave as if nothing was wrong.

As Princess Elizabeth – now Queen Elizabeth II, but unaware of it – returned into the lodge, Michael Parker slipped around the side to attract the attention of Philip through a window.

Philip came outside, where Parker whispered the message from London. The private secretary was to recall later: 'He looked as if you'd dropped half the world on him. I never felt so sorry for anyone in all my life.' He returned inside and told Elizabeth she was now Queen. She had been Queen for several hours – but how long will never be known. The exact timing of her Accession cannot be fixed because no one was with George VI when he died.

HISTORY WILL have to be satisfied that she knew she had become Sovereign at 2.45 in the afternoon, Kenyan time – 11.45 in the morning 4,000 miles away in Britain. She was twenty-five years old and the first monarch to ascend the Throne abroad since King George I succeeded Queen Anne in 1714.

By all the accounts of those close to Elizabeth at the time she took the news calmly. Her training and preparation for this moment came to the fore.

She took command of the situation, signing the documents of her Accession which, as in the North American tour, had been thoughtfully taken along in the luggage. She then sent telegrams to Australia and New Zealand apologising for having to cancel her visit.

Official telegrams and messages began to arrive, making it clear where her duties lay. They were couched in courtly politeness, but it was evident that she was not to be allowed to suffer her grief in private like a member of any other family. She was now Elizabeth the Queen, and, as such, she had to be seen to rule as soon as possible.

All the Royal Family carry around with them, at home or overseas, a suitcase which they hope they will never have to open – it contains mourning outfits. They are included in the luggage ready to wear should they have to dash back to London on receiving the news of a Royal or stateman's death.

Philip had them unpacked and ordered the staff to arrange a quick flight home. Everything was settled speedily and Queen Elizabeth began the journey back to her Kingdom within an hour.

Meanwhile, in London, when the Prime Minister, Winston Churchill, was told of the King's death early that morning, he sat in bed, gazing at the walls of his room, tears in his eyes and scarcely able to speak. When the old Churchill spirit had recovered, he said: 'I really did love him. His advice was so good and I could always count on his support in times of difficulty. I hardly know Princess Elizabeth, and she is only a child.'

The 'child,' Her Majesty Queen Elizabeth II of Great Britain and Her Dominions, together with her Consort, Philip, and entourage, flew through the night via Libya to begin her reign. She arrived back at Heathrow Airport at four o'clock on the afternoon of Thursday, February 7. She walked alone, dressed in black, down the steps of the aircraft to where Churchill and her other Ministers stood waiting with heads bowed. 'This is a very tragic homecoming,' she told them.

From the airport she drove to the centre of her capital and down the Mall for the first time as Queen to Clarence House. At 4.30 a limousine drove slowly out of the gates of nearby Marlborough House. Inside was Queen Mary. 'Her old Grannie and subject must be the first to kiss her hand,' she said. As she curtseyed to her grand-daughter, the new Queen's Royal Standard was raised on the roof of Clarence House.

That night Churchill broadcast an oration which was to be compared with his finest wartime speeches. Mainly in tribute to the dead King, but he recalled that Elizabeth was the name of England's greatest Queen.

He ended: 'I, whose youth was passed in the august, unchallenged and tranquil glories of the Victorian era, may well feel a thrill in invoking once more the prayer and the anthem, *"God Save the Queen"*.'

Queen Elizabeth II was proclaimed at 11 o'clock on the morning of February 8, 1952 on the balcony of St. James's Palace, next door to Clarence House. St. James' is the 'official State Palace'. For example, new Ambassadors are accredited to the Court of St. James'. Kings of arms, heralds and pursuivants in their medieval uniforms gathered with the Earl Marshal of England, the Duke of Norfolk. A fanfare of trumpets heralded Garter King of Arms, who read the following Proclamation to the crowd:

'Whereas it hath pleased Almighty God to call to His Mercy our late Sovereign Lord King George the Sixth of Blessed and Glorious Memory by whose Decease the Crown is solely and rightfully come to the High and Mighty Princess Elizabeth Alexandra Mary; We, therefore, the Lords Spiritual and Temporal of this Realm, being here assisted with these of His late Majesty's Privy Council, with representatives of other members of the Commonwealth, with the Principal Gentlemen of Quality, with the Lord Mayor, Aldermen and Citizens of London, do now hereby with one voice and Consent of Tongue and Heart publish and proclaim that the High and Mighty Princess Elizabeth Alexandra Mary is now, by the Death of our late Sovereign of Happy Memory, become Queen Elizabeth the Second, by the Grace of God Queen of this Realm and of all her other Realms and Territories, Head of the Commonwealth, Defender of Faith, to whom

Her lieges do acknowledge all Faith and constant Obedience, with hearty and humble Affection; beseeching God, by whom Kings and Queens do reign, to bless the Royal Queen Elizabeth the Second with long and happy years to reign over us.'

He raised his hat and shouted, *'God Save the Queen!'* Gun salutes were then fired in Hyde Park and at the Tower of London.

'God Save the Queen' was cried again from town hall steps throughout the Commonwealth as the official proclamation was made. A new Elizabethan Age had begun, four hundred years after that magnificent period in British history.

In the Throne Room at St. James's Palace, the young Queen held her first Privy Council. The impression she made on those one hundred seasoned veterans was striking as, dressed in deep mourning, she moved with quiet dignity to the Throne. There was said to be hardly a dry eye among them as, unfalteringly, she read her Royal Message.

Later in the day the new Queen joined her family at Sandringham and walked with her mother and sister behind her father's coffin as it was borne to the Church of St. Mary Magdalene, across the park from the house. On February 9 the King's body was taken by train to London for his lying-in-state in Westminster Hall, where more than 300,000 people queued in bitterly cold weather to file past his coffin.

Among the callers at Clarence House had been the widowed Queen. The Queen Mother had to bow to the new Sovereign. She was desolate with grief but she kept her feelings hidden. Protocol demanded that she sent a message to the millions around the world who shared her sadness: 'Your concern for me has upheld me in my sorrow and how proud you have made me by your wonderful tributes to my dear husband, a great and noble King.

'No man had a deeper sense than he of duty and of service, and no man was more full of compassion for his fellow men. He loved you all, every one of you, most truly. That, you know, was what he always tried to tell you in his yearly message at Christmas; that was the pledge he took at the sacred moment of his Coronation fifteen years ago.

'Now I am left alone, to do what I can to honour that pledge without him. Throughout our married life, we have tried, the King and I, to fulfil with all our hearts and all our strength the great task of service that was laid upon us. My only wish now is that I may be allowed to continue the work we sought to do together.

'I commend to you our dear daughter: give her your loyalty and devotion; in the great and lonely station to which she has been called. She will need your protection and love. God bless you all; and may He in His wisdom guide us safely to our true destiny of peace and goodwill.' *Elizabeth R.*

After the statement had been published it was noticed that an omission had been made. There was no mention of Queen Elizabeth II's Consort or the two children. Officials hastily set the record straight by phoning newspaper editors to tell them that the reference to the new Queen should have read: 'I commend to you our dear daughter; give her your loyalty and devotion. Though blessed in her husband and children, she will need your protection and your love in the great and lonely station to which she has been called.'

Elizabeth was pleased to notice that the 51-year-old Queen Mother refused to allow sorrow to overcome her. Within a day of her husband's death she was playing with her grandchildren. 'I have got to start sometime and it is better now than later,' she told an aide. There was a moment of anguish before the funeral when Prince Charles asked the Queen Mother when Grandpa was coming back to play soldiers with him. The widow hugged her grandson and could not answer. The three-year-old Prince noticed that his nurses were in tears and said softly: 'Don't cry, Granny.'

Now that her daughter reigned, she was the second lady in the land. She still had the status of a queen and was still referred to as Her Majesty.

Royal visitors, heads of state, dignitaries from all over the globe converged on London for the King's funeral, which was an event of pageanty and martial splendour. The King's coffin was escorted through the streets of London by four Royal Princes – the ex-King, Edward VIII, now the Duke of Windsor, his younger brother, the Duke of Gloucester, his nephew, the Duke of Kent, and his son-in-law, the Duke of Edinburgh.

Queen Mary did not attend the funeral. As the cortège passed Marlborough House, the Queen Mother, the Princess Royal and Princess Margaret leaned forward in the Irish State Coach to catch a glimpse of her. The King was buried in St. George's Chapel, Windsor. On the coffin rested a wreath of white orchids, white lilies and white carnations from the Queen Mother. A card read: *'For darling Bertie, from his always loving Elizabeth.'*

The Royal couple, with Prince Charles and Princess Anne, moved into Buckingham Palace almost immediately afterwards. It was decided that Queen Elizabeth the Queen Mother and Princess Margaret would live in Clarence House. The Queen and the Duke of Edinburgh occupied the Belgian Suite on the ground floor, which is now used by visiting Heads of State. One of Elizabeth's first major decisions in the early months of her reign was to declare clearly once and for all the position of her husband. On September 30 it was announced: *'The Queen has been graciously pleased by Warrant bearing date the 18th instant to declare and ordain that His Royal Highness Philip Duke of Edinburgh... shall henceforth upon all occasions... except where otherwise provided by Act of Parliament have, hold and enjoy, Place, Pre-eminence and Precedence next to Her Majesty.'*

One of the immediate effects of this would be that her husband would be the first, after the Archbishop of Canterbury, to swear allegiance to her after the Coronation.

SHE BECOMES QUEEN

ELIZABETH WAS crowned in Westminster Abbey on a rain-swept June 2, 1953. The country was beginning to recover from the Second World War and the Coronation gave Britain the opportunity to demonstrate her imperial vigour to the world.

More than ten thousand Servicemen – a quarter of them 'soldiers of the Queen' from the Commonwealth – marched in the Coronation procession. Two thousand bandsmen, making up nearly fifty bands, provided the music. Sovereigns and rulers from all over the globe came to pay tribute to the girlish figure who was now the head of the greatest group of nations in history. A hundred thousand people braved the wet weather along the streets. Such was the length of the procession that it took forty-five minutes to pass any one spot.

Nearly nine hundred years before, in 1066, William of Normandy confirmed his conquest of England by receiving the Crown in Westminster Abbey. Since then, every sovereign had been crowned in the Abbey. The ceremony was organised by the Duke of Norfolk. Bernard Marmaduke Fitzalan-Howard, 16th Duke of Norfolk and Hereditary Earl Marshal of England (Master of Ceremonies Extraordinary). He was the official organiser of all Royal spectaculars.

Meticulously stopwatched to the tread of martial feet, whether to the muffled throb of funeral music or the blare of happier State occasions, the Duke master-minded the Coronations of George VI and the Queen, three Royal funerals (King George V, King George VI, Queen Mary), the investiture of the Prince of Wales, and Princess Anne's wedding.

The Coronation, the first great public showpiece of the Queen's reign, coincided with news of the conquest of Everest by Sir Edmund Hillary and Sherpa Tensing – a deed of truly Elizabethan splendour. A newspaper headline declared: 'All This and Everest Too.' It was also one of the greyest June days of the Twentieth Century. But the cold and the pouring rain did not keep away the crowds, including many old people who stood all night to catch a glimpse of their Queen. For those who couldn't be there, television captured the pageantry. The Coronation was the first great triumph of the small screen. Many people bought their first sets for the event and two colour films of the Coronation – *'A Queen is Crowned'* and *'Elizabeth is Queen'* – were later shown to millions of people round the world.

On the morning of the Coronation there were ructions at Buckingham Palace because four-year-old Charles was allowed to attend the ceremony, while his younger sister Anne, was told that she would have to stay at home. There were tantrums, but the Queen insisted that Anne, aged two, was too young to go to Westminster Abbey. As it turned out, the four-hour-long service proved too much even for the satin-suited Charles. He watched the Crowning, standing alongside his grandmother, but then he became impatient and noisy. He and the Queen Mother left early.

Coronation fever had gripped the nation for weeks. It was such that the London *Evening Standard* published a special supplement for those pouring into the capital the night before containing advice on how to prepare for the historic day. Lady readers were assured they still had time to check their 'C-Day Scheme'. Stovepipe trousers were recommended as smart and practical; a ballet-length cocktail dress was advised for parties. 'Don't make the mistake of cramming too much food into your bag,' kerb-watchers were warned. 'Thin brown bread-and-butter cress or salad sandwiches are less thirst-making than cake...'

A memo to men advised: 'Fit a new blade ready in your razor tonight... and put an extra collar (semi-stiff if possible) in your wallet.' For those still hoping to buy seats, the paper announced excitedly that third floor window seats in Oxford Street were selling for £10, places near the Abbey £28.

The crowds were the largest London had ever seen. When statistics were finally compiled for the day it turned out that there were 6,873 casualties, ten per cent of them serious ambulance cases. Legs were broken and in their determination to see everything, many people suffered from exposure after spending the night on wet pavements. Child casualties were few but the injuries included soldiers who were nicked by bayonets while turning street corners in tight marching order.

Seating for 110,000 was built along the processional route in addition to seating for 7,000 in the Abbey. A city of tents sprung up in Kensington Gardens to accommodate the troops. Meanwhile, while London slept – or tried to sleep – in tents or on wet pavements, a plain, unescorted van travelled through the night from the Jewel House in the Tower of London to the Abbey. It carried the priceless regalia for the Coronation.

As a security precaution exact replicas of each piece, enclosed in leather boxes, followed the same route with an elaborate police guard. A large amount of the original regalia had been sold by Oliver Cromwell after the English Civil War. New pieces had to be made for the Coronation of Charles II in 1661 at a cost of £32,000.

The Queen Mother, with Princess Margaret, rode to the Abbey in a glass coach and took her place in the front row of the Royal Gallery. She was only the second Queen in British history to watch the Crown being placed on the head of her child. She was said to be 'glittering from top to toe, diamonds everywhere . . . the Queen Mother playing second lead as beautifully as she had played first.'

The Peers and other senior members of State shouted out: 'God Save Queen Elizabeth.' Trumpets sounded a fanfare.

In her Oath, Elizabeth swore to 'govern the people of the United Kingdom and of her territories abroad according to their laws and customs, to uphold law and justice tempered with mercy and to maintain the established Protestant Church.' With her hand on the Bible she went on: 'The things which I have here before promised I will perform and keep. So help me God.'

By this time the heat of the television lights was such that some of her Maids of Honour were beginning to use smelling salts, concealed in their white gloves, to stop from fainting.

The Oath was followed by her Annointing. This was a sacred practice deriving from the Old Testament account of the annointing of Saul and David by Samuel. She removed her diamond headband and crimson train. Her gown was covered by a plain white overgarment. She was escorted to King Edward's Chair where, shielded by a silken canopy held over her by four Knights of the Garter, the Archbishop of Canterbury said three times, '. . . be thou annointed, blessed and consecrated, Queen over the Peoples, whom the Lord thy God hath given thee to rule and govern.'

For this ceremony he took the oil from the golden Ampulla and used the silver-gilt Annointing Spoon, the two oldest items of regalia which were probably used in medieval coronations. The eagle shape of the Ampulla symbolised imperial power.

The Queen and her escorts then walked slowly to the side of the main altar into St. Edward's Chapel, where she put on a white tunic and a rich golden robe. This was in preparation for her Investiture with the outward symbols of her worldly power. Seated in King Edward's Chair, she was handed the Golden Spurs, symbolizing her adherence to the Code of Chivalry. If she had been a man, they would have been attached to her heels. Instead she just touched them.

Next came the Sword of State and the Jewelled Sword, symbolic of the Sovereign's intention to punish evil-doers. The Archbishop fastened on the Queen's wrists the Armills, bracelets symbolising sincerity and wisdom. The Golden Stole and Robe Royal were put on and the Queen received the Orb. The Orb with Cross, a golden ball surrounded by a jewelled metal band topped by a jewelled arch with a cross, is the emblem of independent sovereignty.

Then on her finger went the Coronation Ring, set with a sapphire and ruby cross of St. George, symbolising the wedding of the Monarch to her people. The climax of the Investiture was the Crowning. The congregation rose as the Archbishop took St. Edward's Crown from the altar and placed it upon Elizabeth's head. A shout of 'God Save the Queen' was heard. The princes and princesses, peers and peeresses could now put on their own coronets and caps. Trumpets sounded and a salute of guns was fired at the Tower of London three miles away.

Now it was time to receive the Homage of her peers, led by her husband. Each knelt before the Queen and promised to 'become your liege man of life and limb.' The Queen then retired to St. Edward's Chapel, where she removed the Royal golden mantle and was arrayed in a robe of purple velvet trimmed with gold – the sign of a crowned and consecrated monarch.

The heavy St. Edward's Crown was exchanged for the lighter Imperial State Crown. Holding the Sceptre with the Cross in her right hand and the Orb in her left, she emerged from the Chapel and made her final stately procession out of the Abbey.

Culmination of the long, three-hour ceremony was when the new Queen, wearing her Crown of State, went out to the Gold State Coach to the sound of ringing bells and cheers.

At the end of the most important day in her life, after a 90-minute coach ride through excited streets and hailing her new subjects from the Palace balcony, she summed up her feelings in a broadcast to the Commonwealth. She told the millions listening: *'As this day draws to its close I know that my abiding memory will be not only the solemnity and beauty of the ceremony but the inspiration of your loyalty and affection.'*

Queen To The World – page 129

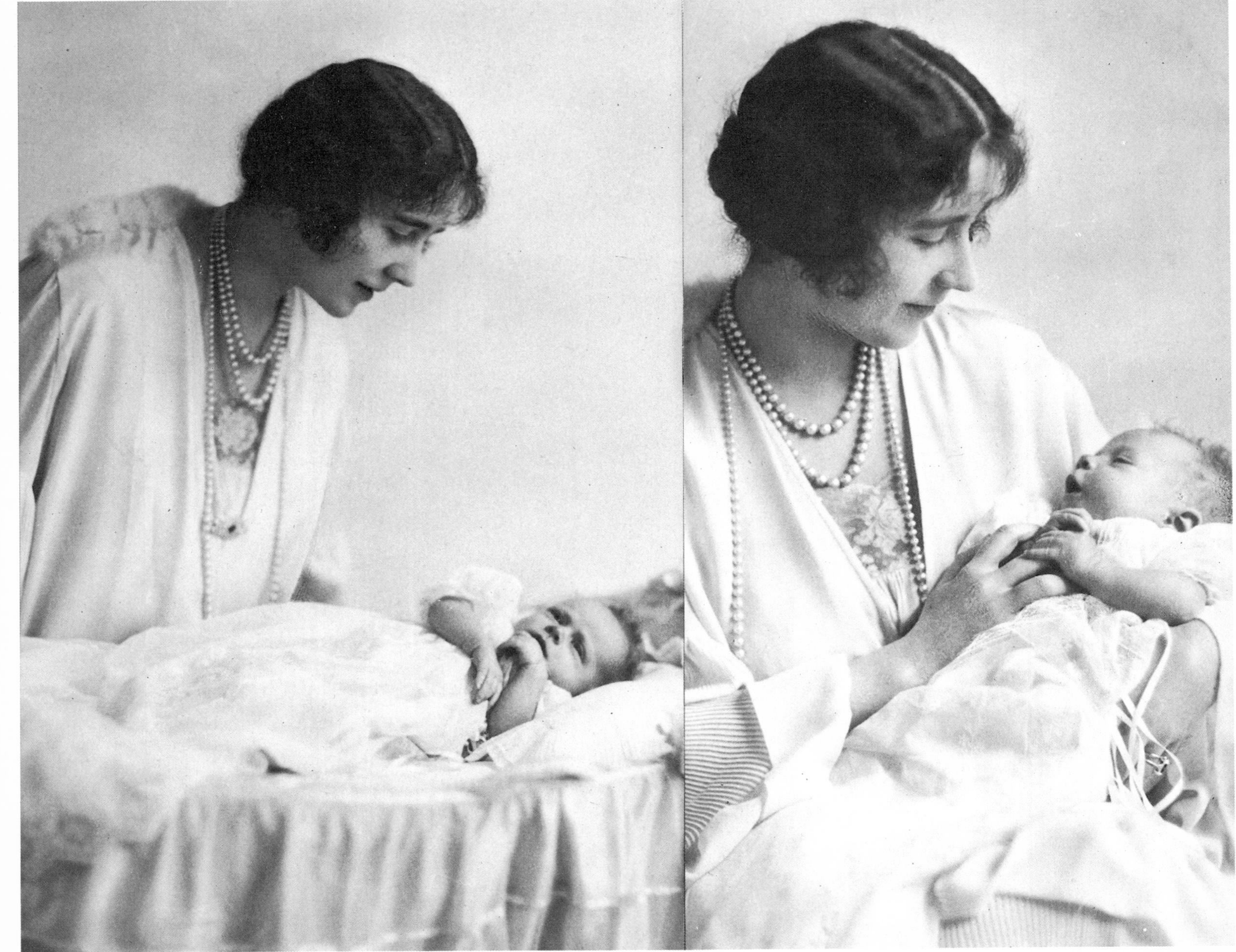

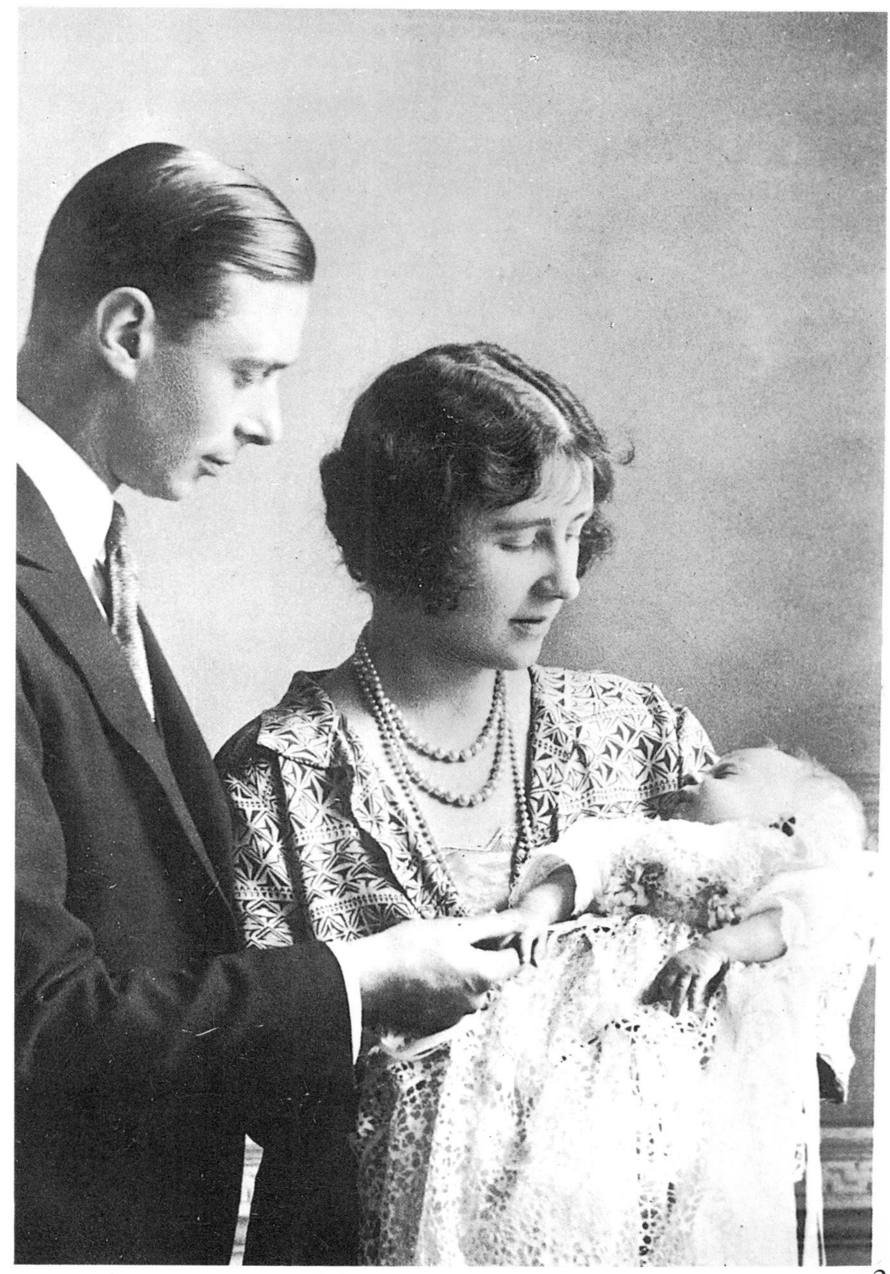

Left, the very first picture of Princess Elizabeth of York taken only a few weeks after her birth, being lovingly cared for by her mother, the Duchess of York.

Above, the christening of Princess Elizabeth Alexandra Mary in 1926. Front (left to right), Lady Elphinstone, Her Majesty the Queen, the Duchess of York and baby Elizabeth, the Countess of Strathmore, Princess Mary and Viscountess Lascelles. Back row, the Duke of Connaught, His Majesty The King, the Duke of York and the Earl of Strathmore. Right, the Duke and Duchess of York with baby Elizabeth.

Above, young Princess Elizabeth (top left) shortly after her first birthday in 1927, and with her father, the Duke of York. A merry smile from young Princess Elizabeth (left) at the age of one as she pauses with her grand-mother Queen Mary.
Top right, Princess Elizabeth at the age of two with her mother the Duchess of York and (bottom) a smile from the young Princess for her father the Duke of York.

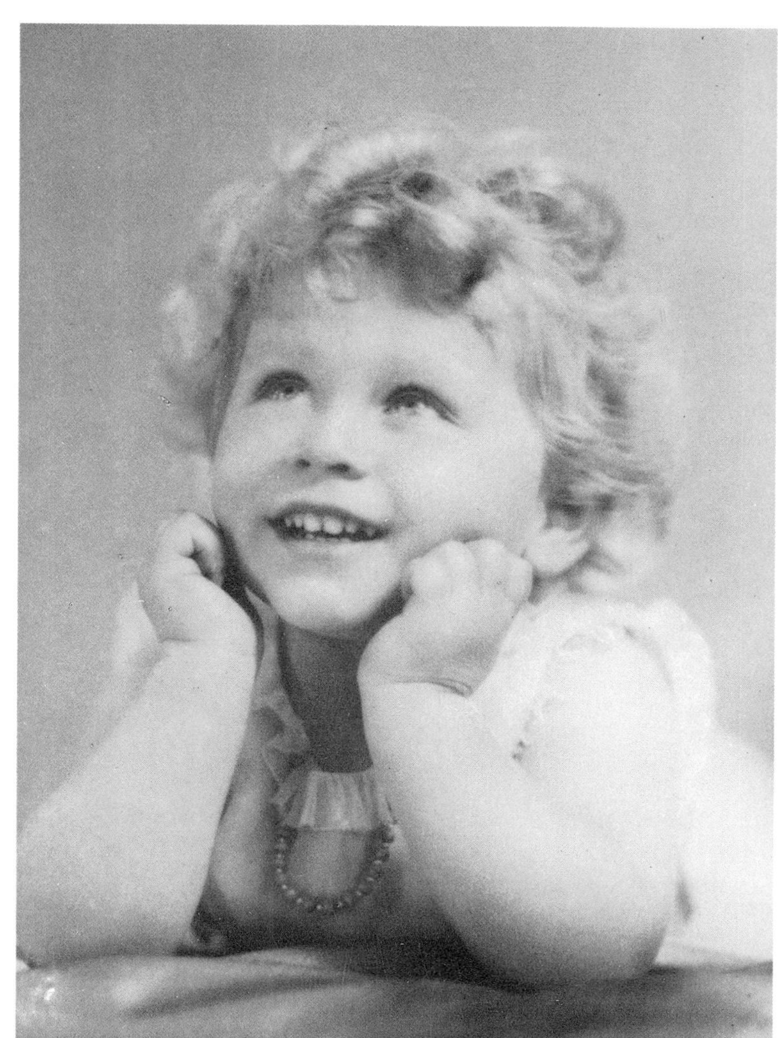

Top: Princess Elizabeth making sand castles at Craigwell House, Bognor, in 1929. Above: the Princesses Elizabeth and Margaret playing in a sand pit. Right: Family photographs of young Princesses Elizabeth and Margaret with their parents, the Duke and Duchess of York, taken in 1931.

Left, Princess Elizabeth with her sister Princess Margaret Rose plays with a rocking horse and afterwards, big sister still keeps an eye on little sister. Later... a helping hand with Margaret's first pony. The pictures were taken in 1932. Above, young Princess Elizabeth shows her early love for animals, while right, the young Princess, in the sort of children's portrait that was fashionable in 1931-32, shows off her crisp organdie dress and carries a daisy in each hand, and (extreme right) Princess Elizabeth one year later.

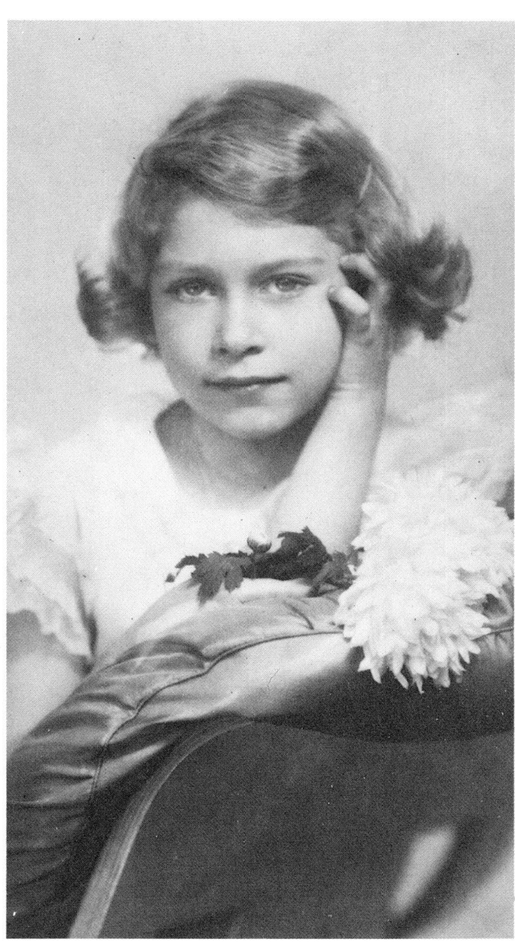

Princess Elizabeth and Princess Margaret could play "houses" in their little Welsh cottage in the grounds of Royal Lodge, inviting Mummy and Daddy for tea-parties served at a knee high table.

“Y Bwthyn Bach” is a miniature cottage presented to Princess Elizabeth and her sister, Princess Margaret Rose, by the people of Wales in 1931. The little house with the straw roof is a child-size, two storey cottage, a complete home scaled down in every detail to juvenile proportion where the adults have to kneel. It has been a source of pleasure to all Royal children since.

A charming study (right) of Princess Elizabeth with her mother the Duchess of York and Princess Margaret taken in 1934. Above, the two Royal sisters.

The years spent at Royal Lodge, Windsor, were among the happiest of her youth. Princess Elizabeth is seen here enjoying a beautiful summer afternoon with her parents, sister Margaret and an army of family pets.

The war is looming, but this charming picture of King George VI and Queen Elizabeth with their young children, the Princesses Elizabeth and Margaret, taken at Buckingham Palace in 1939, warmed the hearts of the nation. (Right) the Royal Family photographed one year later at Windsor Castle on the eve of Princess Elizabeth's fourteenth birthday.

Young Princesses Elizabeth and Margaret photographed in the grounds of Windsor Castle with their mother in July 1941. They spent most of the war years at Windsor (and overleaf).

Sisters together in a moment of calm at Windsor during the early days of World War Two. Above painting lessons with watercolours at Royal Lodge in June 1940.

Princess Elizabeth and Princess Margaret at Windsor Castle – with one of the corgi pets showing very little interest in their studies...

Opposite, there were no kings or queens in this pack of cards when the two Princesses played a word game, one afternoon at Windsor Castle in the same summer of 1940.

Princesses Elizabeth and Margaret Rose (left) are the two stars of a Christmas pantomime at Windsor Castle and (above) the two Royal sisters photographed in 1942.

L

4

Top left, King George VI, Queen Elizabeth, Princess Elizabeth in ATS uniform and Princess Margaret inspect the engine of an army car during the war. Bottom left, Princess Elizabeth learns how to change a wheel. Right, Princess Elizabeth photographed in 1943. Below. V.E. Day scene at Buckingham Palace with, left to right, Princess Elizabeth, Queen Elizabeth, Sir Winston Churchill, King George VI and Princess Margaret waving to the crowd from the balcony.

A traditional British Sunday afternoon finds Princess Elizabeth and Princess Margaret relaxing with their parents in the beautiful gardens of Royal Lodge, Windsor, on a hot summer's day in 1946.

A very informal picture (above) of Princess Elizabeth conversing with her father, King George VI, at Royal Lodge, Windsor, in the summer of 1946, and (right) the Royal Family pause in the beautiful gardens of Royal Lodge.

The engagement of Princess Elizabeth to Lieutenant Philip Mountbatten, 26, was announced on the 10th July 1947, a few months after Princess Elizabeth came of age. The charming studies on the left of Princess Elizabeth and her fiancé were taken at Buckingham Palace on the day of the announcement. The photograph above shows Princess Elizabeth with Lieutenant Philip Mountbatten and Princess Margaret at Buckingham Palace.

Pictures on the left show the wedding of Princess Elizabeth to Lieutenant Philip Mountbatten, Duke of Edinburgh, a title conferred on him the day before by King George VI, who gave away the bride.

The picture above shows the bride and bridegroom leaving Westminster Abbey after their wedding on the 20th November 1947.

In the Throne Room of Buckingham Palace, the bridal couple pose (below) with their immediate family, bridesmaids and pages. The Queen's wedding dress was designed and made by Norman Hartnell, and was in ivory duchess satin, the full skirt embroidered with a corn and rose motif, and worn with a 15 foot long train and white tulle headdress held in place with a diamond and pearl tiara.
Centre: HRH Princess Elizabeth and HRH Prince Philip; on Princess Elizabeth's left: 3rd Marquess of Milford Haven; Lady Pamela Mountbatten; Lady Mary Cambridge; HRH Princess Alexandra of Kent; HRH Princess Margaret; Lady Carolyn Mountagu-Douglass-Scott; Lady Elizabeth Lambert; Miss Diana Bowes-Lyon. Pages: left, HRH Prince William of Gloucester; right, HRH Prince Michael of Kent.
Front row, left to right: Queen Mary, the Queen Mother; Princess Alice, mother of Prince Philip; HM King George VI; HM Queen Elizabeth, the Dowager Marchioness of Milford Haven.
Left: The young couple after the wedding.

Right: The Royal couple, with best man and bridesmaids respond to the warm acclaim from the crowd outside Buckingham Palace.

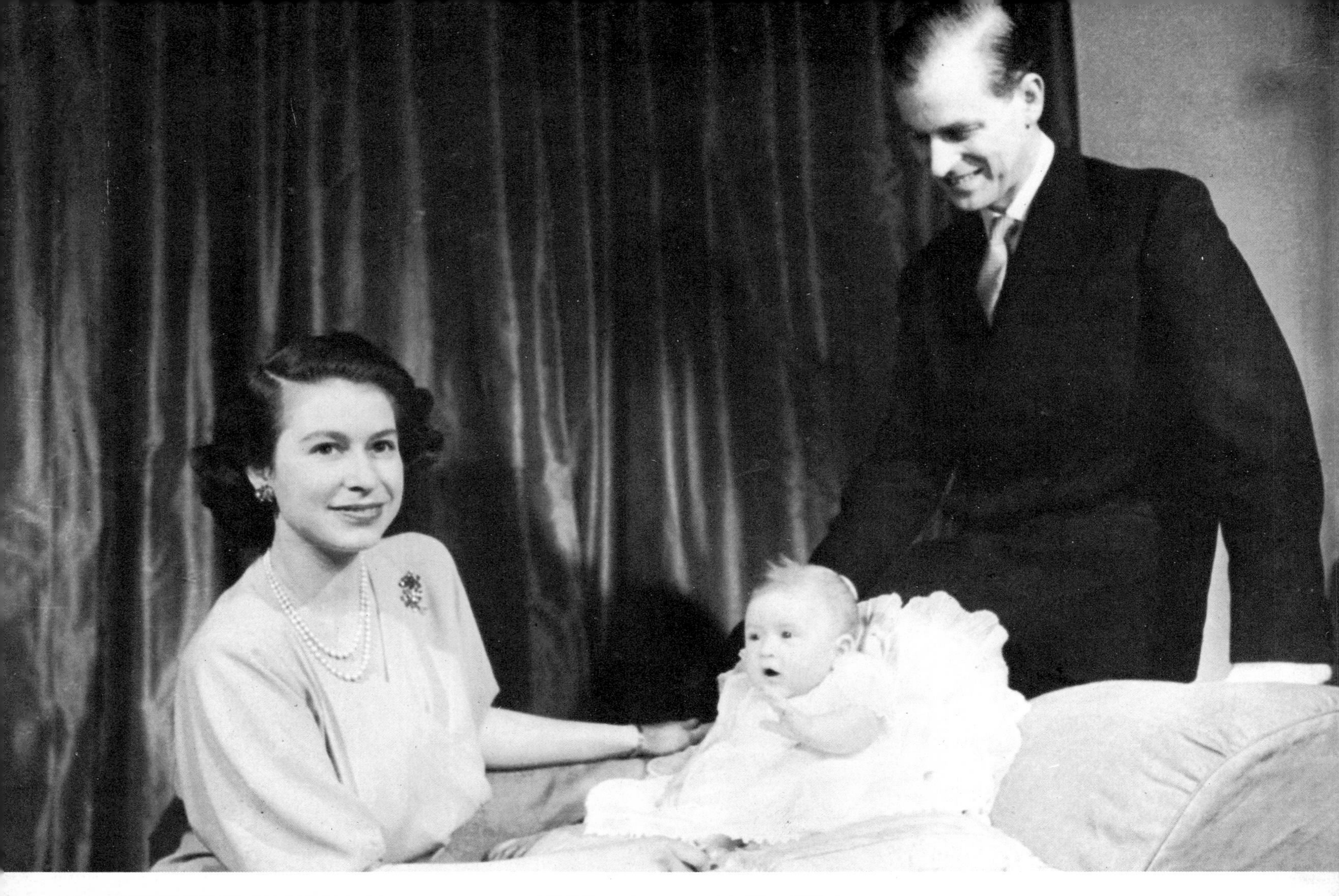

The first informal pictures of Prince Charles taken in Princess Elizabeth's private sitting room at Buckingham Palace, with his parents and (top right) the proud parents after Prince Charles's christening, his first family group picture, and (bottom) proud mother and son.

Above, the first picture of Princess Anne when she was one month old with her mother Princess Elizabeth in the sitting room of Clarence House, and (left) the proud parents pause with the little Princess after her christening.

Top right, Prince Charles with his mother when he was one year old and (extreme right) one month old.
Opposite, The Royal parents with their children, Prince Charles and Princess Anne, in the gardens of Clarence House.

Above, The blissful years. A young married couple with two delightful children. Prince Charles and Princess Anne, photographed in the Drawing Room of Buckingham Palace. (Right) Queen Elizabeth playing with her young children, Princes Andrew and Edward.

A HOLIDAY AT BALMORAL IN 1952... Above, The Queen with Prince Charles driving his pedal car and Princess Anne pushing her toy pram. Top right: The Queen and Prince Charles are at hand to help Princess Anne climb into one of the windows of Balmoral Castle – Prince Charles tried by himself but has to be helped by The Queen. Bottom right: A successful climb is rewarded with smiles all round, and later, The Queen and her children spend a more relaxing moment in the grounds of Balmoral Castle.

Flanked by the Bishop of Durham, on her right, and the Bishop of Bath and Wells, the uncrowned Monarch walks towards the altar in Westminster Abbey for the Coronation ceremony (left).

The moment of crowning (below) by the Archbishop of Canterbury as she sits in St Edward's chair.

Now a Queen. On her head she wears St Edward's Crown – the Crown of England.

Top right, The Queen, seated upon the Throne and wearing the Crown, holds the Royal Sceptre, ensign of kingly power and justice, and the Rod with the Dove, Rod of equity and mercy. Right: The Duke of Edinburgh kneels on the steps to pay homage to his wife.

Above, with her train held by her maids of honour, Her Majesty walks down the aisle of Westminster Abbey to face the crowds outside. Right, the moment of Her Majesty becoming The Queen is over. Now she is surrounded by the Peers in their traditional role of guarding the Sovereign. Overleaf, the Coronation ceremony in colour.

Top left, The Queen with her ladies in Waiting and posing after the Coronation. Bottom, The Composite showing the St. Edward's Crown, The Imperial State Crown and the Head of the Sceptre with Cross. Above, Cecil Beaton's famous Coronation picture of the Queen. Previous pages, The Queen and Prince Philip in Coronation regalia, and the triumphant return to Buckingham Palace.

Above, Queen Elizabeth II at Balmoral Castle playing with Prince Charles in the summer of 1952. Right, Her Majesty the Queen with her children, Prince Charles, playing with his pedal car, and Princess Anne.

Charming family photograph of Her Majesty The Queen with Prince Philip and their young children Prince Charles and Princess Anne taken in the beautiful grounds of Windsor Castle.

Above (top left) Her Majesty The Queen holds her fourth child Prince Edward on the balcony of Buckingham Palace after Trooping The Colour. (top right) The Queen holds Prince Edward after a walk in the grounds of Windsor. With her is Prince Philip, Princess Anne and Prince Andrew. Above, The Queen drives Prince Charles and Princess Anne to Windsor. Right, the Queen and Prince Philip with the children in the gardens of Windsor Castle.

Above, the Queen with her family

Opposite, a family lunch at Windsor Castle.

The Queen and Prince Philip with their children at Windsor Castle, and (right) with Prince Philip reading through the volume of Royal mail.

Top left, the crowning of Prince Charles as Prince of Wales at Caernavon Castle and (opposite) a Christmas family picture at Windsor Castle. Above, the Queen with the Queen Mother and Princess Margaret watch the competition at the Badminton Horse Trials.

Overleaf, the Queen with the Queen Mother and the Duke of Beaufort "roughing it" at the water jump at the Badminton Horse Trials.

A hound from the Duke of Beaufort's pack steals an honour usually reserved for the privileged few when it "kisses" her Majesty's hand at the Badminton Horse Trials. (right) The Queen presents rosettes at the Windsor Horse show.

Left, the Queen presenting Princess Anne with a prize at the Windsor Horse Trials. Left bottom, a coach ride with Prince Philip at the Ascot races. Above, a family group in the unsaddling enclosure at Ascot.

The Queen holds baby Prince Edward (top left), and (above), photographed in the Blue Drawing Room of Buckingham Palace, Her Majesty with her two month old Prince Edward and four year old Andrew. (Left) The Queen with her two younger children at Euston Station departing for Balmoral. (Opposite) The Queen and her family photographed at Buckingham Palace.

SCOTLAND

Her Majesty the Queen drives in the Scottish State Coach (below) en route to St Giles Cathedral for a service for the Order of the Thistle of which the Queen is Sovereign, and, wearing the robes of the Order, the Queen and Prince Philip leave St Giles Cathedral after the service.

Above, undeterred by the pouring rain, the Queen arrives for the Ghillie's Ball at Balmoral Castle, during the celebrations of her Silver Wedding. Below, the Queen, with Princess Margaret and Princess Anne, make a most delightful picture, and (right) the Queen dances the night away.

Bad weather does not deter Her Majesty the Queen who enjoys long walks on the hills of Balmoral, and here she clearly revels in the Great Outdoors.

Her Majesty enjoys taking her dogs for long walks and responds to their playful mood. The charming family photographs show Her Majesty the Queen with her immediate family at the time of her Silver Wedding. With her at Balmoral are Prince Philip, Prince Charles, Princess Anne, Prince Andrew and Prince Edward.

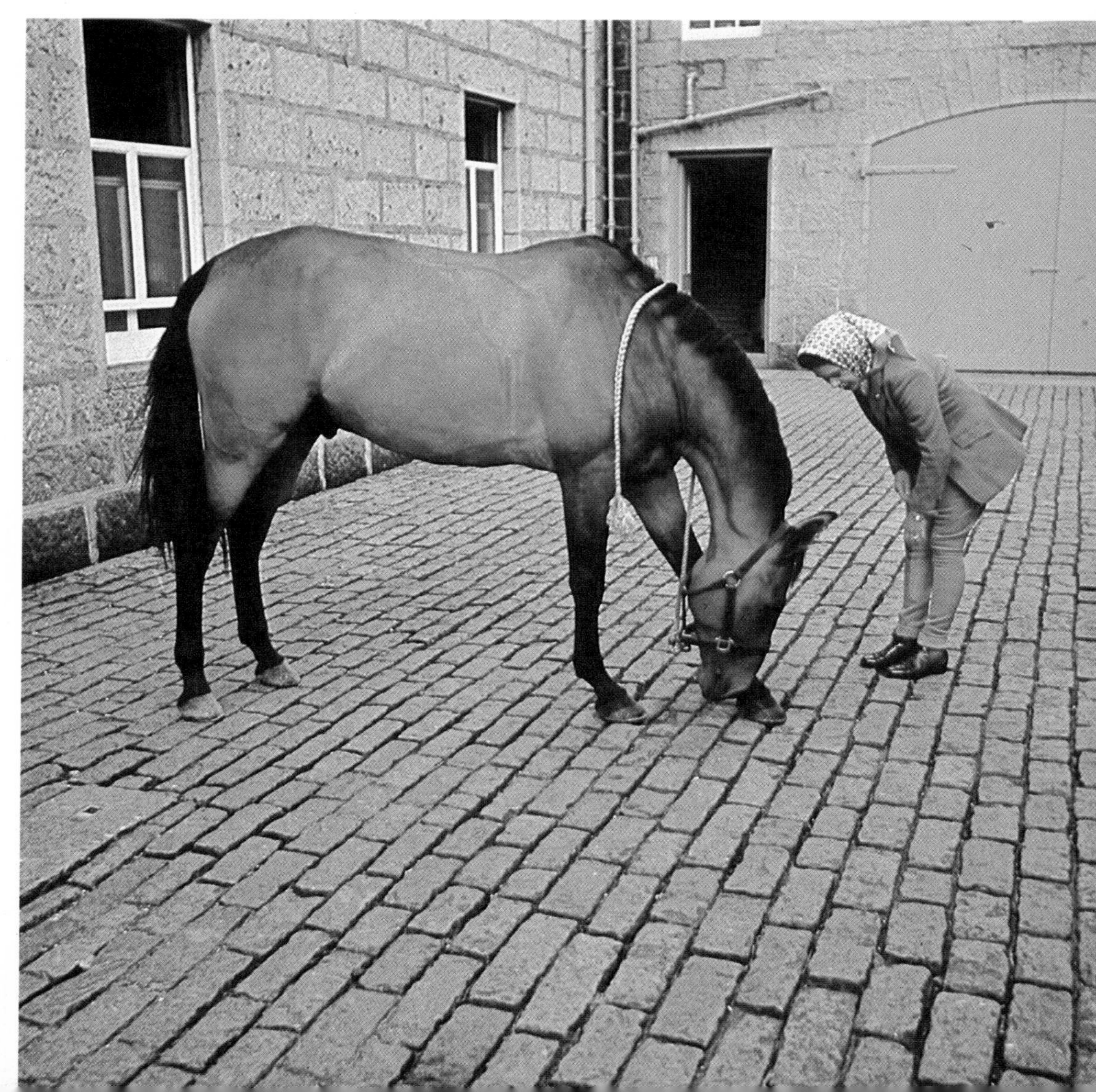

Whenever the Queen is able to relax in the country, it is almost certain that there will be animals with her, particularly dogs. This lovely picture of the Queen, right, sitting by a waterfall in the castle grounds, features two of her corgis – Tiny is on Her Majesty's knee and Brush at her feet. And horses. Above, she is pictured riding Cossack in the grounds of Balmoral Castle, the Queen's much loved Scottish home, which can been seen in the background.

The Queen, with Prince Philip, Princess Anne and the late Duke of Norfolk at the Epsom Derby in the early 1970's.

The Queen and Prince Philip conversing with Princess Anne before a competition in Windsor Great Park.

The Queen with her family (left) and above with the late Duke of Beaufort watching the cross country event at the Badminton Horse Trials from a hay cart.

First wedding in the family. Captain Mark Phillips, a commoner who changed the style of Royal marriages, and Princess Anne in the drawing room at Buckingham Palace (above) after the Westminster Abbey service.

Opposite (top) the solemn moment when they exchanged their vows, and (below) when Mark experienced for the first time the traditional family 'get together' on the balcony of the palace.

A general view of Princess Anne's wedding at Westminster Abbey.

QUEEN TO THE WORLD

ROYAL TOURS ABROAD

ALMOST IMMEDIATELY after her Coronation it was decided that Her Majesty should show herself to her subjects overseas. In 1953, she became the first monarch to fly the Atlantic when she went away for 173 days on her first Commonwealth tour. In Australia she covered 2,500 miles by train, 900 by car, 10,000 by air, made 102 speeches, listened to 200 more and stood to attention for at least 162 varied renderings of the National Anthem.

The Queen has always set herself an exhausting pace on her trips around the Commonwealth. During the Silver Jubilee celebrations of 1977, it was of her own choosing that she wanted to meet as many people as possible on Commonwealth walk-abouts. In the first five days of her 14-day tour of New Zealand – where she introduced the practice seven years earlier – she notched up ten walk-abouts, the first just two hours after stepping ashore.

In Auckland, 900 luncheon guests had to be kept waiting because the Queen was on the streets with her people. In New Zealand she flew 1,818 miles to 26 cities, towns and villages. In Australia, she spent 20 hours in the air, flying 6,218 miles in 707 jet-liners and Royal Australian Air Force planes. She was off among the Australian people only thirty minutes after flying into the federal capital, Canberra.

And these 'Down Under' schedules were followed by ceremonies and receptions in the South Pacific islands of West Samoa, Tonga and Fiji.

The Queen knows better than any of her advisers that whenever she comes into close contact with her people, there lies danger. But she is a modern monarch, and looking at the world through the glass windows of Royal carriages or bullet-proof cars is not her way.

Sir Martin Charteris, the Queen's Private Secretary, said during the Australian and New Zealand tour: 'The Queen is happiest when she is walking among the people in a country town. She is a country person at heart.' Security men were worried by demonstrators at one stop-over but, as Sir Martin said, 'She was neither upset nor worried – it would not cause her to travel in a closed car.'

By this time she was 51 and looking 'weary' to some sympathetic observers. They said there were times when the formal mask slipped and the tiredness spread across her face. Journalists accompanying her suggested just one typical day alone would have worn out an athlete, let alone a slightly-built, middle-aged woman. One morning she inspected old people's homes in Sydney, unveiled a plaque, and then flew one hour forty-five minutes to Launceston, Tasmania.

She went on a walk-about, met local representatives, and two hours later took a thirty-five minute flight to Hobart. She attended an official function, saw a military tattoo and finished her day at 11.00 p.m. Between stops she still had to carry out her full-time duties as the Queen. The telegrams and the official papers still flooded in.

One of the most important tours from the point of view of political links and trading potential was the 1979 cruise around the Persian Gulf, when she flew out to board *Britannia*. It proved to be one of the most successful the Queen has ever made. In Saudi Arabia there was the problem of how to greet a woman in the land of purdah. She was designated an 'honorary gentleman'. Her ladies-in-waiting, Lady Susan Hussey and the Duchess of Grafton, were also allowed to attend the Queen, but long dresses had to be worn and necks, elbows and ankles covered.

Elsewhere on the trip, at the White Palace in Doha, Qatar, the Queen took tea with the Emir's senior wife, Sheikha Roda, who told her how the four wives were rotated in the order in which they were married. The seventeen-year-old newest wife, Sheikha Mooza, stayed in the back-ground with her two babies.

In October 1982 the Queen flew to the Pacific again for what was one of the most colourful of her many overseas visits. The first stop was Australia, and was like any other tour of that country, except that its emphasis was on the Commonwealth Games which the Queen, with Prince Philip, spent much of her time watching. Brisbane played host to her with massive welcomes everywhere, and a succession of memorable engagements.

A reception at the Queensland Cultural Centre followed a spectacular firework display when the Queen arrived by barge down the Brisbane River. She stayed on to close the Games, then moved on to Canberra where, on a walk-about, hundreds of children spoke or gave flowers to their Queen.

The Royal pair then spent a fortnight visiting six South Pacific Commonwealth countries – including Tuvalu, Fiji, Papua New Guinea and Nauru. The use of *Britannia* gave the Queen and Prince Philip the bonus of two or three days' rest at a time as they sailed from one country to another. Colossal feasts and tribal dancing awaited the Royal visitors everywhere.

In Tuvalu the islanders brought the Queen and Prince Philip ashore in canoes and carried them through the streets to the centre of Funafuti, to the sound of singing. In Papua New Guinea, she and Philip renewed their acquaintanceship with the famous mud men – fierce warriors who cover their faces with mud masks. The natives of Papua did not quite understand Prince Philip's status so they called him 'Number one fellah belong Missus Queen'.

I found out what goes on behind the scenes in organising a Royal Tour during the State Visit to Japan in 1975. Behind the cheers, the smiles, the bows and the waves were six years of patient effort, thousands of hours of work by diplomats and the Queen's personal staff. It all started on a small scale in 1969, after Emperor Hirohito was invited to London. It was a great international exercise, involving Buckingham Palace, the British Embassy and the Japanese Foreign Ministry.

They faced the sort of nightmare that happens every time the Queen travels. On the Japan trip she brought a personal staff of thirty, including four secretaries, two dressers, two maids, six footmen, a hairdresser, two ladies-in-waiting, her Private Secretary, Sir Martin Charteris, her Assistant Private Secretary, Mr. William Heseltine, her Press Secretary, Mr. Ronald Allison, and her Medical Officer, Surgeon Commander Philip Fulford.

Then there was her Equerry-in-Waiting, Major Robin Broke, and the Captain of the Queen's Flight, Air Commodore Archie Winskill, who organised all the air travel. Prince Philip had his own Equerry-in-Waiting, Major Henry Hugh Smith, and his own valet.

Two Scotland Yard men, Chief Superintendent Mike Trestrail and Inspector Chris Hagan of the Metropolitan Police guarded the Royal Couple. Lord Shepherd, the Lord Privy Seal, was acting as Prime Minister Harold Wilson's representative. Lady Shepherd was with him, and so was a private secretary.

As the Queen and Prince Philip moved along, Surgeon-Commander Fulford stayed close carrying a list of specialists along the way who could be called upon at short notice, and his bag containing drugs and bandages for immediate first aid. Hospitals on their route were warned to stand by with plasma and blood in the Royal Couple's groups.

Before the Queen reached Japan, Allison, the Central Office of Information Press Officer, and the British Embassy in Tokyo, sent out 5,000 pictures of the Royal Couple, published more than fifty different handouts and brochures on the Royal Family and Britain, and distributed more than 100,000 ft. of television and cinema films.

In January 1975 five members of the Queen's staff flew to Japan to go over the programme with the Japanese and the British Ambassador, Sir Fred Warner. As Allison said: 'It had to be organised so that everything would go smoothly. Her Majesty needs to have plenty of staff around her because at least two hours each day are still spent dealing with official papers.'

QUEEN ELIZABETH is not only Head of the Commonwealth but official 'glad hander' to the rest of the world, so the guests she entertains cover a huge cross-section. State visits by the heads of other nations usually have considerable political and trade significance, and Her Majesty is required to play her part. Britain and the United States still have a special relationship, no matter how fragile it appears at times, based on common origins and institutions. Therefore, when President Ronald Reagan and Mrs. Nancy Reagan paid an official visit in the summer of 1982 it was a happy occasion in which to re-cement the old friendship between the two countries.

It had the usual round of official banquets, but such is the magic of the Royal merry-go-round that world attention focussed to an astonishing degree on a delightfully relaxing interlude when the President joined the Queen for a ride through Windsor Great Park one sunny morning.It was the fairy-tale start to President Reagan's first day in Britain, and could easily have been a scene from one of the films he made as an actor years ago...

There was the sun, rising through the morning mist to the East of Windsor Castle, providing the perfect lighting effects for a beautiful English summer's day; there were the colourful characters playing 'bit parts' the red-uniformed Grenadier Guards in bearskins standing sentry at the Castle's imposing George IV Gate; uniformed Berkshire policemen smiling and waving and generally giving a very good performance of friendly British bobbies; American security men prowling beneath the ramparts; relaying mysterious messages through their short-wave radios.

All this... and a Scottish piper playing a lament

from the historic Past, swiftly followed by the sound of the Present – high-flying jets dipping in salute.

Enter stage left the Queen's new Press Secretary, Mr. Michael Shea, who solemnly told a motley assortment of 'extras' masquerading as the British and American media that, despite portraying many a cowboy in his old films, the President did not eat baked beans for breakfast before the day's ride. That fascinating and absorbing snippet of information duly delivered, it was the turn of Lieutenant-Colonel Sir John Miller, the Crown Equerry, to take the stage and explain that Mr. Reagan would not be riding with a Western saddle. 'We have one or two here but Mr. Reagan asked for the British Eastern saddle, which is the sort in regular use,' he said.

Then ACTION, CAMERA, and off they set, the Queen in jodhpurs, hacking-jacket and head-scarf, riding one of her favourite horses, Burmese, which she usually uses for Trooping the Colour. The President, likewise in jodhpurs and a beige jacket that looked as if it had spent its better years rounding up cattle on his ranch in California, sitting astride eight-year-old Centennial from the Queen's stables.

Following behind in a carriage was Prince Philip and Mrs. Nancy Reagan, the whole scene in slow motion as the procession drifted around the sweeping general path in front of the gate, the President, despite his 71 years, riding tall in the saddle as he chatted with the Queen. They in their turn were shadowed by security men and the Press, who coaxed a few impromptu lines out of Mr. Reagan as he rode into the sunrise!

'How do you like your horse sir?' – *'Beautiful'*.

'Does it ride well?' – *'Yes'*.

He joked with reporters standing behind a waist-high barrier: *'If you stand back, I will take it over the top.'* At this comment, as if on cue, the Queen moved off and Mr. Reagan followed.

During her 1983 return tour of the United States, the Queen was said to be in 'sparkling form' at an official banquet in San Francisco. She made President Reagan roar with laughter when she referred to the storms which had plagued her visit to California: 'I knew before we came that we have exported many of our traditions to the United States. But I did not realise before that weather was one of them.'

And as the laughter dried away she added: 'But if the climate has been cool, your welcome, and that of the American people, has been wonderfully warm.' In America, the pace had turned hectic and soggy with one Pacific storm after another smashing into California. Her Majesty had to take a battered Navy bus through flooded Los Angeles freeways and a perilous ride through cascading waters on a mountain road to the Reagan ranch. She saw the tinsel of Hollywood and the sophstication of San Francisco, where protest demonstrations happily fell far short of their threat. Her bodyguard of 230 secret service agents, plus many local police at every stop, was considered necessary given America's record of violence.

The Queen remained calm, alert and interested throughout a schedule that left officials and journalists exhausted in her wake, though she confided to an American television reporter that she looked forward to putting her feet up at the end of Royal Tours.

There were armed police everywhere in the St. Francis Hotel, where the Queen stayed in San Francisco. They packed into the hotel's lobby, jostling with hotel guests, sealing off exits, checking out the kitchens, even standing on chairs to observe her arrival. The City had never seen such tight security arrangements, hastily stitched together, when it was announced that the Queen would be staying. The local police chief said it was the city's biggest operation of its kind ever. Nothing was left to chance. Even the manhole covers around the hotel were welded to ensure that no intruder could make his way into the Queen's bedroom.

The 79-year-old hotel coped with the Royal Visit with an appearance of outward calm. The Queen was given the hotel's $1,100 (£725) a night Presidential Suite, with its two bedrooms, two bathrooms, gas fire-place and six telephones. The masculine decor was softened by replacing the red leather furnishing with lighter gloss upholstered chairs and sofas, and by bringing in mirrors and lots of flowers. As the Queen entered the hotel for the first time, Mr. Frank Elliott, who played the piano in the lobby bar, broke into a jazzy rendition of *'God Save the Queen'* because, he said, 'it seemed a pleasant idea'.

Shortly after the San Francisco banquet, the Queen and Prince Philip went off to spend a weekend in the solitude and splendour of the Yosemite National Park in California where, standing at Inspiration Point, she was able to look down the spectacular valley. Locals have a saying that it takes two men and a boy to take in the view... certainly, as anyone who has been there knows, you can see for miles.

But the peace and tranquillity were shattered by the deaths of three U.S. Secret Service men assigned to the Royal Couple. This clearly upset the Queen, who looked stunned when she arrived at her hotel in the Park on Saturday.

The three were killed when their car was in collision with a sheriff's car on its way to join the Queen's motor convoy. They were in the second of a three-car convoy filled with agents heading for the Park, where they were to go on duty later in the day. News of the accident was flashed to the Queen's convoy about twenty-five miles away, and the vehicle carrying her redirected along a parallel route. However, the wreckage of the smashed car was clearly visible and an ambulance still at the site when she passed the scene.

Her visit was part of a five-nation tour which began in Jamaica, where the welcome was summed up in a calypso that ran: '*Long-time Gal we never see Yuh*' – despite three previous visits. In the tax haven of Cayman Islands, Telex messages about shifting money went unheeded for a few hours while everyone vied for places to see the colony's first Royal Visit.

The Royal arrival in Mexico was regarded throughout Latin America as gently helping to renew British influence in the region after the Falklands War.

The trip ended in Vancouver, where she received armfuls of flowers from the children of British Columbia. '*Britannia* looks like a floating flower shop,' said the Queen at a farewell banquet given by Canadian Prime Minister Trudeau the evening before her departure. Mr. Trudeau told her: 'You represent those qualities of character and dedication, that resolute spirit and concern for others which Canada and Canadians need in these difficult times.'

After only 5½ hours' sleep, the Queen left Britannia for Vancouver Airport and the flight home in a Canadian Forces 707 jetliner. As she went on board, wearing a brown fur coat against the dawn chill, she received yet more flowers from children.

She was back in Canada again the following autumn for an exhausting two-week tour that ended in Manitoba before going off to the States... this time for a holiday. Before she left she was reassured by Mr. Brian Mulroney, the new Prime Minister, of the Monarchy's importance in his country's life. His remarks were made at a farewell dinner for 1,600 guests in the Winnipeg's Convention Centre. 'You have carried out your difficult and onerous duties with a warmth and charm that have endeared you to Canadians everywhere,' he told the Queen. 'The Monarchy is a central feature of our national life and of our parliamentary democracy,' he added to loud applause.

The Queen, in her reply, pledged herself to continue serving as Queen of Canada. 'The Crown was able to act as a unifying and distinctive symbol of nationhood during the formation of Canada. The crowds of people of all ethnic origins and denominations who gave me such a warm welcome ... demonstrated that this symbol still has a real value.'

She then spent eight marvellous days on two magnificent ranches, horse-riding much of the time. Senator Malcolm Wallop, brother-in-law of Lord Porchester, her racing manager, said before she arrived to stay with him: 'I am hoping to give the Queen a really relaxed holiday – she certainly deserves one. Here she will ride and walk and do just as she pleases. It's going to be a hundred per cent no-fuss holiday.'

The Queen slept in a huge bedroom with a picture window overlooking mountains covered with pine forests, where she was able to spot deer, wild turkey and grouse. Her other stop was at the splendid ranch home of US breeder John Galbraith at Lexington, Kentucky. Mr. Galbraith owned the Darby Dan Stud Farm, which housed one of the Queen's mares, Round Tower. When she arrived in Lexington she was introduced to the new foals.

Her Majesty's friendship with John Galbraith began in 1972, when his horse, Roberto, won the Derby at Epsom with Lester Piggott on his back. Mr. Galbraith, who is a great fan of the Queen, was also determined that she would enjoy her stay. 'The Queen is a charming, charming woman,' he declared. 'Why shouldn't she have a holiday and enjoy the same rights and privileges and freedoms as anybody else?'

THE ONE EVENT of any year that allows the Queen to reach all her subjects at home and overseas virtually instantly is the famous Christmas Broadcast.

The Royal tradition was started – reluctantly – by King George V, who was asked to use the microphone by Lord Reith, the first Director General of the BBC, in 1923. He wrote to the King's private secretary: 'Such a personal message (at Christmas) from His Majesty to all sorts and conditions of people in town and country districts alike would make, in these difficult and anxious times, a national moral impression, the effect of which could hardly be estimated.'

The King refused that year, and every other year, until 1932 when he agreed to make a short speech on Christmas Day. Now it is not only broadcast world-wide but watched on television at home in Britain by 25 million people at the set hour of three in the afternoon.

In addition, around seventy tapes are flown to radio and television stations throughout the Commonwealth. French Canadians hear it in French, the BBC Overseas Service translates it into scores of languages from Urdu to Japanese, and news agencies wire it to thousands of newspapers. But one clichéd phrase has vanished. 'My husband and I' was changed to 'Prince Philip and I' and today it is usually 'our family'.

She once broadcast the Christmas message from New Zealand, when she said: 'I want to show that the Crown is not merely an abstract symbol of our unity but a personal and living bond between you and me.'

There have been sad moments during her travels among cheering crowds, songs and dances. Such a one I witnessed when the Queen and Prince Philip made a State visit to France in the early summer of 1972. Towards the end of the tour and after visiting Longchamp race-course, she, her husband and Prince Charles travelled a few miles to the home-in-exile nearby of the dying Duke of Windsor, old Uncle David.

As I saw them greeted at the door of the mansion at 4 Route du Champ d'Entrainement by the Duchess of Windsor, it was still not certain that they would be able to see the seriously ill former uncrowned King Edward VIII. The Duke had been receiving cobalt therapy for a cancerous tumour – without any success.

After serving tea in the drawing-room, the Duchess took the Queen upstairs alone to see the Duke. He was in a wheelchair, dressed in a blue blazer that hung loosely on his body. He weighed little more than six stone. As Her Majesty came in the Duke stood up with great difficulty, said, 'My dear', made her a slight bow and kissed her on both cheeks.

Seeing the strain that a simple act of rising from the chair had caused, the Queen insisted that he must sit down again. Prince Philip then came in, followed by Prince Charles. The Duke began a coughing fit, so the Queen, Philip and Charles went downstairs with the Duchess.

Those of us waiting in the garden of the house were unaware of how seriously ill the Duke had been. First hint came when only the Duchess came out to pose for pictures with Her Majesty and her family. It had been arranged originally by the British Embassy in Paris that the Duke was going to join the photo session. It would have been an historic picture. A former monarch, a ruling monarch and a future monarch together. Three generations of Royalty.

The Duke, alas, was not up to it. The Queen hid her innermost feelings with an air of smiling normality. Ten days later the Duke of Windsor was dead.

Sorrow on another occasion, also in France, twelve years later when the Queen talked to British D-Day widows, sharing their pride and sadness among the tombs of their husbands in Bayeux Cemetery. She summed up everyone's feelings when she stopped for a word with 65-year-old Elizabeth Jenkins beside the long rows of headstones, testimony to the terrible losses forty years earlier.

'Such dreadful tragedies, weren't they?' said the Queen quietly. Mrs. Jenkins, from Southampton, nodded. Her husband, Robert, was killed in action, trying to save his comrades. It was a poignant moment in the immaculate Second World War graveyard, where 4,648 British soldiers, sailors and airmen are buried. The party of 53 widows, who were nearly left out of the anniversary celebrations, were flown by the Defence Ministry to Normandy in time for the commemoration ceremony at Bayeux attended by the Queen, Prince Philip and President Mitterrand.

The widows sat in two rows near the Cross of Sacrifice, where the Queen laid a wreath of blood red roses. Ten thousand people were at the service. For many, the sounding of the *Last Post*, followed by an eerie silence broken only by the distant barking of a dog, was too much. Old soldiers, some standing to attention and others crippled in wheelchairs, cried as they remembered their dead comrades.

Afterwards the Queen, in turquoise suit and matching hat, moved among the widows and veterans, chatting, smiling, comforting. She told Mrs. Violet Butler, 63, from Chiswick, West London, that she thought the service had been very moving.

The Queen then spoke to Chelsea pensioner, George McKenzie, from Edinburgh, who was wounded, captured and escaped – all by 7 a.m. on D-Day. He was an orderly in the Royal Army Medical Corps. Somehow he managed to hide a knife before he was searched, and killed a guard. The Queen told him: 'I have heard of your exploits. You're an old hero, aren't you?' George's face crinkled with pride.

Mrs. Barbara Bruford, from Marshwood, Dorset, said: 'To me this service has meant so much. The Queen has been marvellous. It is a memory I shall keep for ever.'

Her Majesty had arrived earlier at dawn in the Royal Yacht, passing under Pegasus Bridge almost on the hour that the 6th Airborne Division made its drop there forty years ago. The *Britannia* made a spectacular sight in the morning mist against a pink and gold sky. Later, the Queen lunched aboard the Royal Yacht with King Baudouin of the Belgians, Queen Beatrix of the Netherlands, King Olav of Norway, and the Grand Duke of Luxembourg.

For long distance travel, the Queen usually flies in a British Airways jet-liner. Short-hop work is carried out by 32 Squadron of the R.A.F. using three propeller-driven Andovers of the Queen's Flight which are nearly twenty years old, slow and have limited range. They are frequently piloted though, by Prince Philip and Prince

Charles, whom I have seen make some very tricky landings with great skill in bad runway and weather conditions.

Although there are helicopters in the Queen's Flight, she does not like travelling in them. But there was one occasion when she had to go by 'chopper'. That was during the Silver Jubilee tour to Northern Ireland, when it was the only secure way to get her from the Royal Yacht around the province.

By contrast, the Queen Mother is very fond of helicopters. She was the first member of the Royal Family to travel in one in 1956, when she flew from Windsor to Biggin Hill. She is supposed to have said that the 'chopper' transformed her life, 'as it did of Anne Boleyn'. It was time-saving and exciting, enabling scheduled engagements to be spread farther afield.

HER MAJESTY'S SECURITY

THE QUEEN'S 'walkabouts', the way she mingles easily and freely with the crowds waiting to greet her wherever she goes, gives her enormous satisfaction. She loves them. Her security men are terrified of them for her sake.

For threats on her life, which have never materialised as real attempts, go back almost to the start of her reign. Most are from cranks.

But there has been a disturbingly consistent catalogue of violence which has built up in recent years. In 1974 there was the armed kidnap attempt on Princess Anne in the Mall. In 1977 a placard was thrown at the Queen as she drove through Sydney, narrowly missing her face. Later that year in London, outside the Albert Hall, her car was showered by eggs. In 1978 a man was fined for swearing at her outside a West End cinema.

Three years later, in 1981, a bomb exploded at Sullom Voe oil terminal in the Shetland Isles while the Queen was on a visit. She was nowhere near the blast, for which the Provisional IRA claimed responsibility. In the summer of 1981, six blanks were fired at her by a teenager as she was riding to the Trooping of the Colour. It spooked her horse, Burmese, and she had to keep a tight rein on him as he jumped and shied.

On the day of the Trooping the Colour, Her Majesty had just reached the junction of the Mall and Horse Guards Approach Road when the youth fired at her. Behind her were Prince Charles and Prince Philip. Suddenly the Queen saw, just ten feet away, a figure point a black revolver at her. There was nobody in front or beside her to protect her. There were six shots, two spaced and the rest bunched. Prince Charles and the Duke of Edinburgh rode up and closed in on her. 'Are you all right?' asked Philip. 'Fine,' she answered and went on calmly with the parade.

A Scots Guards hero of the moment, Lance Corporal Alistair Galloway, told later how he nearly stabbed the youth, Marcus Sarjeant, with a bayonet. Lance Corporal Galloway was standing on ceremonial guard duty in the Mall with bayonet fixed when the shots rang out. 'When I turned and saw the man holding the gun I felt hatred,' he said. 'There was raw anger and, with the Northern Ireland training, I wanted to get him. I thought of using the bayonet on him.'

Galloway, a quiet-spoken Scot from Huntly, Aberdeenshire, described what happened: 'I was at the present arms. The Queen was about seven yards away. There was a noise which I thought was the crowd clapping – then I recognised it as gunfire. It sounded like a nine millimetre. I turned round and saw this man pointing a gun at the Queen. As I turned he fired the last shot. The crowd were shouting and he was being pushed forward.

'I leaned across the barrier and grabbed him by the hair. I never saw the gun after that. He was on the ground and the police came and took him away. Some of the crowd clapped. But no one said anything to me. I think people think of us as glorified dummies when we are on ceremonial parade. Now they know we are soldiers. We are there to protect the Queen.'

A year later an unemployed man in his twenties, Michael Fagan, slipped through the Buckingham Palace security system and found his way into the Queen's bedroom. He spoke to her when she awakened, and she coolly kept him in conversation while she summoned help.

The Queen's protectors are a special squad of the Metropolitan Police, who are armed now in a way that was never considered necessary just a few years ago. They would be much happier if she would let them place more positive barriers between her and the public. Clearly she must be more closely protected, but it remains inconceivable that the Queen and her close family change the very nature of their existence by exchanging the open State coaches for bullet-proof limousines and retreating behind glass screens.

But the protective screen, often invisible, is never let down by the men guarding her. For wherever the Queen goes anywhere in the world she is protected between countries by the RAF or the Royal Navy... sometimes both, working together. Nowhere was this cover, involving detailed and intricate planning, better demonstrated than on her flight to India via the Gulf States in 1983. A Nimrod four-engined jet, normally used to shadow Russian subs and planes, was with the Royal plane all the way to the Northern end of the Gulf, when another Nimrod, operating out of Singapore, took over.

That way there was constant radar surveillance, and in seconds both planes could whistle up the RAF's latest fighters flying out of Cyprus, or friendly states within the Gulf.

Not that she ever saw them, but they were there, sitting just over the horizon, keeping a watch, within spitting distance but never visible. In any case, the Queen has a dislike of such obvious heavy protection. On board the Royal plane is a special channel linked up via a military satellite and keeping it in constant touch. As a Royal pilot put it... 'When I am flying down-route as skipper, without the Queen, it can sometimes be a long job contacting London. When I am flying the Queen it is like picking up a phone to ring the next room; the connection is almost instantaneous.'

No chances are taken when it comes to guarding the Queen, not even with the friendliest of nations. Our military just do not rely on others to do their job. Whenever she flies to America, for instance, she is escorted either by the RAF or Canadian forces.

There are other on-board precautions. It was felt for example that special steps had to be taken to protect her against terrorist missile attacks when she flew to the Middle East in March 1984 on a State Visit to King Hussein of Jordan.

The wide-bodied Tri-Star 500 carrying the Royal Party had already been fitted with devices to detect ground or air-launched missiles – and deal with them. The fear was that the Queen's Flight could be the target for shoulder-fired Sam 7 anti-aircraft missiles.

So missile detection systems were installed as part of the Tri-Star's 'refit'.' The other key component, an anti-missile device, was taken on board nearer to the departure date. It was designed to deal with anti-aircraft missiles in one or two ways. First, by firing flares on which missiles will home instead of the aircraft jets. Second, by showering strips of metal foil into the air to confuse a missile's guidance system.

According to the editor of *Jane's All the World's Aircraft*, Mr. John Taylor, at the time: 'It's not novel for a passenger aircraft to carry an anti-missile system of this sort. It is a fairly normal precaution taken when airlines fly on delicate jobs carrying important people who might attract the attention of terrorists.'

Fears for the Queen's safety arose because of the murderous feuding among Arab terror groups. Hussein's position on the question of Palestine meant he – or his guest – could be thought a target by some.

But Her Majesty just gets on with the job, appearing to give little thought to the worries of the security men around her. Twice in the United States in 1983, for example, she surprised US Secret Service agents by leaving her car with Prince Philip to shake hands with people cheering and waving Union Jacks in Seattle. At one stage the Queen was only fifty yards from half a dozen people shouting, 'Brits out of Ireland.' She smiled at people in the crowd and pointed towards the small band of demonstrators, to the horror of US security officials, who had been attempting to dissuade dignitaries from going into crowds since President Reagan was shot in Washington two years earlier.

But the atmosphere in Seattle was very relaxed compared with the earlier heavy security precautions in San Francisco, where every footstep of the Queen and Prince Philip had been dogged by US Secret Service bodyguards. Some of the biggest crowds seen during the US visit, running into many thousands, were able to get closer to the Queen in Seattle than had been possible in other US cities, where cordons kept them back, often as far as 100 yards.

How serious are the dangers the Queen faces were horrifyingly demonstrated six years ago with the brutal murder of Lord Mountbatten, his 14-year-old grandson and a teenage friend by Irish terrorists. It happened when a bomb, planted on his fishing boat, was detonated by a radio signal as he sailed near his holiday home in the Irish Republic.

The Queen was on holiday at Balmoral when, on August 27, 1979, she heard on the radio the news that invoked world-wide condemnation. Her Majesty immediately drove over to nearby Birkhall, the Queen Mother's Deeside home, to comfort her. The assassination of her 79-year-old 'Uncle Dickie', put the British Royal Family in the front line of terror targets.

The entire family rallied round. At first they found it hard to believe that the unthinkable had happened. It was a terrible blow for Philip and Charles, both of whom had been so close to Mountbatten nearly all their lives. When the funeral took place at Romsey Abbey in Hampshire, the wreath from Prince Charles had the message, 'To my HGF and GU' – to my Honorary Grandfather and Great Uncle.

By all accounts, Elizabeth and those near and dear to her have never got over the circumstances of his death, one of the greatest tragedies in their lives. Even today they find it hard to keep their emotions bottled up when they read of a pro-IRA demonstration, or see television pictures of terrorist funerals in Ulster.

FAMILY MATTERS

SIMMERING IN THE background during Coronation Year was a family problem that just would not go away. Princess Margaret was in love – not only with an unsuitable commoner but, to make matters worse, a divorced man. He was Group Captain Peter Townsend, whom the Queen Mother had appointed as Comptroller of her Household. Previously he had loyally served as an equerry to King George VI.

As a Battle of Britain pilot, Townsend had been decorated for 'outstanding leadership... in aerial combat.' King George had made him an Equerry of Honour. He eventually became Deputy Master of the Household. Royal duties imposed a strain on his marriage and in the autumn of 1952 Townsend divorced his wife. When Mrs. Townsend had remarried shortly afterwards, Princess Margaret thought she and Townsend could now marry. But the tenets of the Church of England on divorce prevented Margaret marrying him and the Queen, as head of the Church, could not give her consent.

Attitudes have changed since Margaret wanted to marry Townsend, but thirty-five years ago everything seemed to be against them. He was a commoner, he was more than fifteen years her senior, and he had already been married and had children.

The Queen Mother was very fond of Peter Townsend and appointed him to her own household after King George VI's death. She is still friendly towards him and they have met occasionally over the years since the enforced breakup of his romance with Margaret.

The Queen and the Queen Mother were in favour of Margaret finding happiness with Townsend, but the Government and other Royal advisers were against the match. The powers-that-be insisted that the affair had to be ended. Townsend was sent abroad to a forced exile lasting more than two years. The two lovers were kept apart but they continued to exchange letters and phone calls.

A few weeks after Margaret's twenty-fifth birthday, the Queen Mother brought the pair together again at her London home, Clarence House. She left them alone for the evening to see if they could resolve their problem.

Apart from Townsend's unsuitability as a prospective husband, there were also other snags to their relationship. If Margaret went ahead and married the man she so desperately wanted, she would have to renounce all her rights to the throne, retire from Royal life and forfeit her official 'salary' from the Civil List – worth today £120,000 a year.

Remembering the decision they had to take together, Towsend wrote later: 'There would be nothing left except me, and I hardly possessed the wealth to compensate for the loss of her Privy Purse and prestige. It was too much to ask her, too much for her to give. We should be left with nothing but our devotion to face the world.'

Neither the Queen nor the Queen Mother put pressure on Princess Margaret at this delicate time. They made it clear that she had a free choice. While the mother listened to her younger daughter pouring out her soul hour after hour, she realised that there was only one real decision to be made bearing in mind the attitudes of those days.

With great reluctance, Margaret took the step her friends say she has regretted ever since. On October 31, 1955, Margaret and Townsend were left alone again by the Queen Mother at Clarence House so that they could make their final farewells. An hour later Princess Margaret issued a statement that referred to such matters as 'being mindful of the Church's teaching that Christian marriage is indissoluble.'

It was all dressed up in high-minded phrases, but what really mattered was the sentence: 'I would like it to be known that I have decided not to marry Group Captain Townsend.' The anguish behind the Princess's statement highlighted a Royal problem which grows in complexity with each decade. With the princely and noble houses of Europe almost everywhere else in decay, members of the Royal Family can no longer look abroad either for a marriage partner or an equivalent lifestyle.

Four years after that break, Princess Margaret fell in love with another commoner, fashion photographer Tony Armstrong-Jones. This was a time when photographers did not have the 'In' image they have today and there are some in Royal Circles who claim that Margaret deliberately turned her back on better connected suitors to defy those who had caused her so much heartbreak earlier.

Margaret and Tony used to meet secretly in a small cottage alongside the river in London's dockland. It became their own special home where, among discreet neighbours, they used to have very close friends around for dinners cooked by the Princess on a small stove.

The Queen hoped that this second great love of her sister's life would have a smooth passage. Thankfully it did. All that she had been denied five years earlier came true for the Princess on May 6, 1960 with a wedding in Westminster Abbey that had all the traditional Royal trimmings. Margaret adored her husband and began to enjoy the company of his artistic friends, ranging from fashion designers to film stars such as Peter Sellers and Liza Minelli. Their home in Kensington Palace soon took on a bohemian air with all-night parties attended by the sort of guests not normally invited to Royal homes.

The marriage went well at first, even though Margaret was against Tony making a living and career away from Court circles. He was not prepared just to live off his wife. But after ten years together and despite both being devoted to their two children, their love began to sour. It became an open secret among their friends that they were spending more time apart than together – and causing discomfort to the Queen and the reputation of the family.

With their son and daughter away at boarding schools, the need to stay as a couple seemed unnecessary. Lord Snowdon moved out into a house of his own a mile away and they began leading separate lives. In March 1976 the inevitable happened – they announced they were splitting-up. This was followed by divorce. Lord Snowdon then remarried.

WHATEVER THE OCCASION, the Queen is usually as impeccably dressed, though in a different style, when she is walking the corgis at Sandringham as she is when opening Parliament at Westminster. The long training carries her as faultlessly through the mud as the reception line. Her pleasures and pursuits, whether watching her horses in training or the Badminton trials, demand informal clothes – but they are always perfect for that moment.

The conservative approach, imposed on her by her early background, her discipline and her own rigid sense of propriety, has been a long time dying. It is only within the last few years that she has taken a real interest in clothes, shown a keener sense for fashion, ventured a little more bravely into different styles and received genuine compliments from those who understand fashion.

In the evening she will wear separates, like a silver tissue skirt banded in black velvet with a black velvet top, or a simple tailored dress and high-necked jacket to match in stiff silk, or a shirt-neck evening dress in floating printed chiffon.

Apart from her family, her main interest away from the Throne is training and breeding racehorses, so more than most people she dresses for the outdoors. For the country clothes she buys Daks skirts from Simpsons, which are fitted for her at the Palace, and cashmere sweaters and cardigans from Scotland. She wears headscarves, silk and cotton open-neck shirts, trousers on the Royal Yacht, riding breeches, fur-lined bootees or Wellingtons or brogues, lisle or wool stockings, tweed or camel coats or car coats, and Gannex mackintoshes or Burberry coats.

They have little or nothing to do with fashion and have not altered over the years, either for her or for any other woman; they are almost exactly the same as the tweed suits and sweaters and shoes she wore as a child. For summer there are cotton frocks, often sleeveless, and plain wool frocks and flat-heeled pumps, and yet the string of pearls, the pearl stud earrings and the lapel brooch are almost always present.

Gloves, which are regarded as essential by the Queen, are not only a sign of formality, though rather old-fashioned, but a practical defence for a woman who has, in the course of duty, to shake so many hands. Fine suede (which has to be cleaned) is more elegant, but the Queen prefers gloves in suede fabric, easily washed, easily removed, easily dyed. Furthermore, the time consumed in smoothing on suede gloves is something which she cannot afford.

As unchanging as the style of her gloves are her handbags. Always capacious, always in good quality heavy calf for daytime and sometimes silver tissue for evening, often black but occasionally white, never without a loop to hang over her wrists and never far from her side, they have ignored fashion change and been a frequent subject of criticism. Clutch handbags and shoulder handbags are out of the question, because the Queen must keep both hands free and cannot bother with hitching up shoulder bags.

The enormous size of her handbags has never been explained, for she never has to pay out ready cash, doesn't need the front door key, doesn't smoke, doesn't need a shopping list, doesn't have to pay the grocer's bills out of pocket, and appears to go for hours without renewing her make-up. Although she is almost never seen without her handbag, she is never seen to open it.

In terms of clothes, the Queen has always done her own thing with an incomparable standard of professionalism. Better than most, she is able to live up to the old maxim that a well-dressed woman, having put on her clothes, then forgets about them. Yet, despite her tremendous care and good taste, there can be criticism. The unkindest and most outrageous was during the Royal Tour of Canada in 1984 when Canadian newspapers said the Queen looked old and tired. They accused her of failing to draw the crowds.

The *Toronto Globe and Mail* went further. It criticised the Queen's clothes and make-up and said: 'Her legs have visible veins.' The paper received protest phone calls, including one from a Briton living there who suggested the reporter should be hanged, drawn and quartered. He wasn't joking either, for there was more, much more of the same stuff from the paper.

In a front-page article it said: 'She looks tired at times,' and went on: 'People in crowds say repeatedly, "She looks just like my grandmother." On this tour the crowds weren't even there. 'There is little of the excitement or the ten-deep crowds that greeted the Prince and Princess of Wales.'

And of Prince Philip, the paper said: 'He is sixty-three and has a stoop at the shoulders. The once handsome Greek face is now dominated by bushy eyebrows. He often looks as bored as courtesy allows. He has a tart and unpredictable tone.'

The paper's managing editor, Geoff Stevens, defended its outspokenness: 'It was a very affectionate piece but critical. I thought it was a very good profile of the Royal Couple. It observed that they are getting older, which is a fact of life. I have seen her myself during the tour and I was surprised at how old she is looking these days. I don't think you could term it anti-Royalist.'

The *Toronto Sun* launched a vitriolic attack on the Queen's fashion sense, accusing her of being 'dowdy' and 'matronly', and of her hairstyle commented tartly: 'She looks like she put her head on the pillow and just got up.' While the liberal *Toronto Star* published a piece with the headline '*Has the Monarchy Become Redundant*?'

The Queen's Press Secretary, Michael Shea, refused to comment on the attacks. 'The Queen has always had a very warm welcome in Canada,' he said. He was right in that. British newspapers and fashion experts immediately rallied to her defence. Three out of four people taking part in a newspaper survey disagreed with Toronto newspapers' claims that she looked 'old and tired.'

A massive 95 per cent objected to criticism of her hairstyle. Only 30 per cent thought her clothes were dowdy; 73 per cent thought they were right for her age. Tory MP Anthony Beaumont-Dark, who had just returned from a Canadian visit said: 'I am confident these comments do not represent the view of the Canadian people.'

But then the Queen has weathered other storms in more than a dozen visits to Canada. In 1964 she faced a near riot from a hostile crowd in Quebec city. In 1978 there were snubs by the then Prime Minister, Pierre Trudeau. He was not in Canada to meet the Queen on her arrival – he had been holidaying in Morocco. Later he turned up for a Royal meeting at the Commonwealth Games dressed in a short-sleeved shirt, no socks and open sandals.

The Queen's fashion advisers say that over the years she has developed a look of 'understated elegance' that almost any other woman in her position would find hard to rival. When she chooses a wardrobe for her foreign tours, or official functions in Britain, there are a multitude of factors to consider. Designs have to be practical for walk-abouts, comfortable in extreme temperatures, and photogenic.

One of the Queen's favourite dressmakers, Ian Thomas, said: 'I think she always looks terrific. I make clothes for her and I only make what she likes. She knows what she wants and that is the most important thing. Fashion writers are in no position to criticise her. They are the worst-dressed of the lot. They profess to know all about clothes but at every fashion show they look appalling.'

Before going on a tour overseas she is advised by her wardrobe staff on what to wear. Lists are drawn up of what outfits might be still serviceable and what needs to be made. Next, a couturier produces sketches and prepares a selection of fabrics – usually of pure silk, pure wool or pure cotton. Colours must be bright and clear and the hats must leave the features of the face visible. Make-up, incidentally, must be simple and strong to put over a clear image to photographers and the television cameras.

Fur coats are rarely worn. Her Majesty has a superb collection of furs, including sables and wild mink, but, because of the international campaign against wearing the pelts of rare wild animals, Royal furs are now in cold storage.

Also prepared for taking on a trip is a list of the medals and Orders of Chivalry that the Queen wears on appropriate occasions. They have often been presented by the Heads of State the Queen has visited or she has received at Buckingham Palace.

Among more than forty foreign orders she is entitled to wear are ... the Grand Cross of the Legion of Honour of France, the Collar of the Order of the Nile of Egypt, the Collar and Grand Cordon of the Order of the Chrysanthemum of Japan, the Special Grand Cross with Star of the Order of Merit of the Federal Republic of Germany, the Grand Cross of the Order of the Liberator, General San Martin, of Argentina and the Order of the Supreme Sun of Afghanistan.

An indication of how many changes of clothes the Queen needs can be seen from the following diary I kept when accompanying her on the tour she made to Japan, via Jamaica and Hong Kong, in 1975.

Pulled out of her suitcase each day were different creations by Norman Hartnell and Ian Thomas, who had worked under Hartnell's direction for thirteen years until launching out on his own. All told she took thirty dresses, forty pairs of shoes, four diamond tiaras, a large handcase of jewellery and fifteen hats. That wardrobe fit for a queen filled ten cases for the marathon tour from the West Indies to the Far East...

April 20, 1975: The Queen wore an ochre silk dress overprinted in white for her evening arrival in Jamaica. Collar and cuffs white silk organza. Hat white draped organza trimmed with dress material, white rose.

April 27: Daytime, yellow and white printed shirt-waister dress. White pillbox hat, yellow trimming. Evening dress with short sleeves in pale yellow organza over white. All-over embroidery in multi-coloured sequins and rhinestones.

April 28: Pink linen dress, full pleated skirt. Sleeves, collar, hem bound with white linen. Pink linen pillbox hat, top scattered with white violets, pink bow. Later changed into printed silk dress in yellow, orange and lime. Fitted bodice, pleated front panel. Lemon yellow straw hat, folded back brim. Crown of lemon and orange flowers. Evening dress in blue printed organza with matching embroidery. Sleeves long and flowing.

April 29: Evening dress of deep rose georgette, gold thread embroidery. Separate loose back flowing from shoulders.

April 30: Evening dress pure silk georgette in tangerine and lemon on cream ground. Skirt and sleeves crystal pleated, pressed out at flounced hems.

The Queen spent two days on a private visit to Hawaii. Then it was on with the travelling fashion show...

May 3: The Queen made a brief stop in Guam, wearing a printed silk striped dress of emerald, lime green, turquoise, royal blue.

May 4: She chose printed silk dress in emerald and white for arrival in Hong Kong. Full unpressed pleated skirt, short sleeves and hem bordered with black and white stripes. White silk hat overdraped with emerald organza.

May 5: In the morning the Queen wore same pink outfit as on April 28. At lunchtime she changed into sunshine yellow crêpe dress with three-quarter-length full sleeves. Small cloche hat, trimmed with yellow and white gardenias. She attended an evening race meeting in sleeveless coat of geometric silk printed in blue and green design over chiffon dress in similar printed pattern with small bishop sleeves.

May 6: Morning outfit of orange printed shirt waister dress with sun-ray pleated skirt. Breton hat in hyacinth blue straw. Afternoon, multi-coloured print dress with bat-wing sleeves. Breton hat in pomegranate straw to tone.

May 7: The Queen left Hong Kong in turquoise and white printed silk dress with standaway collar and skirt cut in shaped godets. Hat of white pleated organza trimmed with white and turquoise. She arrived in Japan in a dress of pale green and mauve printed pure silk crêpe de chine, worn under a lilac coat lined with matching print of dress. Green flowered hat. In the afternoon, she changed her hat for a green silk turban.

At a State banquet that evening the Queen wore a thick white silk evening dress, bodice decorated with bands of gold fringe embroidery and each side of skirt having graduated bands of similar embroidery. Diamond and ruby tiara, necklace, cluster earrings and bracelet.

May 8: Shantung dress and coat of heavy cream, both trimmed with wide bands of stitching. Hat of cream straw and cream veiling. Lunchtime and afternoon, dress and coat of turquoise silk organza. Breton-shaped hat in white with brim of matching turquoise silk. For dinner with Japan's Prime Minister, the Queen wore a sky-blue chiffon evening dress with fitted bodice. Kimono sleeves, embroidered with pink organza cherry blossoms, which also decorated the hem of the full skirt.

May 9. Red and white printed pure silk crêpe de chine with white plaited belt. Matching silk coat. Small hat with upturned brim. Evening dress in turquoise chiffon with long sleeves for banquet at British Embassy.

LIFE AT THE PALACE

THE QUEEN IS awakened every morning by Bobo, bringing in a cup of tea and a plate of biscuits handed over by the footman who is not permitted to enter the Queen's bedroom. With Bobo come the corgis, who usually beg to be given the biscuits while Bobo draws back the curtains. But there is a quaint and heart-warming change of roles on Bobo's birthday. Then it is the Queen who brings her maid in the morning cup of tea.

Although more than 80 years of age, Bobo is still an enormous influence on the Queen, and probably knows her better than anyone else in the world. Officially she is the Queen's maid and head dresser. Privately she is a true, loving and loyal friend, who has devoted her life to the

Queen and been with her through the good times and the bad.

Apart from a few months as a chambermaid in a Scottish hotel, Bobo has been in Royal Service all her working life. Wherever the Queen is, it is usually possible to spot her – on the deck of the Royal Yacht, or hovering in the background in each of the palaces or at Sandringham or Windsor. She has special powers and privileges. She lives in a flat directly above the Queen's apartment and has a specially carpeted bathroom. It is said that this former nanny to the mistress who became a monarch is one of the few people in whom the Queen can safely confide.

Where the Queen goes, she goes. Her age has made no difference to her willingness to join Royal tours. Her hair is set by the Queen's hairdresser, and her clothes are made by the Queen's dressmakers and designers. When the Royal hairdresser attends to the Queen's coiffure, he pops down the corridor and attends to Bobo's afterwards.

Bobo makes all the appointments for the Royal couturiers and has considerable say in choice of style and fabric. When travelling, she is always the first person to be served her food after the Queen. This is at the Queen's insistence.

On the anniversary of her fifty years of Royal service, the Queen had a very special commemorative present made for her by the Royal jewellers. It was a brooch made in the shape of a flower and it has 25 diamonds which quiver on 25 gold stamens.

THE QUEEN'S working day usually begins at eight o'clock, listening to the radio and reading the morning papers and personal letters. Breakfast is at nine with Prince Philip and the rest of the family. In the Palace grounds below the window, a bagpiper plays a few cheerful tunes to get the morning moving.

The first paper the Queen turns to is *'The Sporting Life'* – Bible of the horse-racing fraternity. Such is her enthusiasm for what has been called the 'Sport of Kings' that the publishers send a copy by messenger straight from the presses each night. Soon after breakfast she is at her desk in her study, where she works until lunch at 1.00 p.m. She deals with at least 120 letters, delivered to her in white whicker baskets.

They are often crammed with human problems: a desperate mother with a husband in prison and mounting debts; a farmer complaining about roadmakers trying to steal his land; or, perhaps, a schoolboy wanting a medal to be presented to the surgeon who saved his life. Every letter – apart from those from obvious cranks – gets a reply.

Those sent out from Buckingham Palace are typed on special thick paper called 'Original Turkey Mill Kent'. They are easily recognised as they pop through postboxes because the envelopes bear no stamps; instead they are marked with ER, the Royal Insignia. Such is the amount of mail handled at the Palace each day that it has its own post office, which is tucked away in the left-hand corner as one looks at the building from the Mall.

A staff of secretaries jets around the globe with the Royal Family. They tend to be very hard-working, though not especially well paid: dictating letters, making phone calls or hammering away at typewriters, more for the enjoyment and privileges of the job rather than for healthy bank accounts. On overseas tours I have seen them trying to create order out of chaos in the back rooms of palaces as they dash from city to city, country to country. Very often the most they see of their 'boss' or the country they are visiting is by a quick glance at local television between handling correspondence and arranging official functions.

The Queen appreciates the strenuous help she gets from her staff, so she usually says 'thank you' with a private dinner party on the last evening of a tour. The next morning they are busy again bundling typewriters, dictating machines, notepaper, files and other office paraphernalia into cases for yet another dash to yet another airport.

Every day there are also official telegrams and dispatches from all parts of the world, matters of State affecting not only Britain but other nations of the Commonwealth, such as Canada, Australia and New Zealand.

The Queen has an enormous amount of paperwork to deal with each day. No matter where she is in the world, dispatch boxes carrying Parliamentary or diplomatic documents, State briefings, and letters arrive daily. In London the official papers reach Buckingham Palace during the night and early morning by car and still, in this day and age, horse-drawn carriage from Whitehall. When she is abroad they are flown out, no matter where she is staying.

Dealing with official correspondence has to be fitted in between appointments. As much work as possible is done in the morning, but Her Majesty often has to return to paper-work, which sometimes takes her late into the night, after she has shaken the last hand of the day and given a final wave to the crowds.

These papers either inform her of Government proposals, fill in the background of events at home and abroad or seek her signature on legislation. It might be a major Bill or a minor reform overseas but it still needs her signature under the constitution of Britain and the Commonwealth. The Queen must be informed and consulted on every aspect of national life to the widest possible extent. She is also free to put forward her own views in private for the consideration of her Ministers, but the final decision is always that of Parliament. That eminent Victorian, Walter Bagehot, described the sovereign as one who had 'the right to be consulted, the right to encourage and the right to warn.'

She does not merely rubber-stamp a document. She likes to be well briefed about current events and, although she has no power to alter the decisions of her various Parliaments, she insists on knowing exactly to what she is putting her signature. Current Parliamentary activities in Britain are discussed at the regular weekly meeting with the Prime Minister.

Her Majesty's advice and reaction to Parliamentary affairs is frequently sought because of her vast political knowledge. She has been served by eight Prime Ministers – six Conservatives and two Socialists. Her involvement in State affairs has been so rich and varied that Prince Charles has paid tribute to his mothers as a 'repository of vast constitutional and political knowledge.'

If she has no official engagements at mid-day, the Queen helps herself to a light meal served buffet style. Hopefully she would have her husband or one of their children or grandchildren with whom to share lunch. As she deals with her daily intake of paperwork she sits at a desk cluttered with family photographs, paper-knives, a paste-pot and scribble pads. On the carpet nearby is a drinking bowl for her pet corgis, who are usually stretched out watching her every move.

She stops for tea at five, then carries on reading and signing official documents. Dinner is served at 8.15 and when Prince Philip is home they chat away about their respective day's work.

If there are no evening engagements, she will often watch television. The Queen likes comedy shows, documentaries and nature study programmes. She does not stay up too late, however. She likes to be in bed by 10.30.

Speeches for the Queen and Prince Philip are generally researched and written by their staffs, after which they give final approval and perhaps add a few personal touches. Elizabeth is careful not to express any controversial views in public because, apart from sometimes causing too much of a stir, once recorded, her remarks take on a permanency that can become embarrassing for the future. She avoids taking a stand on an issue. Views are often put forward as rhetorical questions rather than statements, for the simplest comments can sometimes cause offence.

Until recently Royal Speeches were written by advisers steeped in Royal service and remote from everyday life. They, not the the Queen, created the oft-ridiculed phrase: 'My husband and I.' In Canada in 1959, she and Prince Philip started a rebellion to exert their own influence over the dictates of their protocol-conscious assistants.

Prince Philip cut out clichés like 'truly great occasions' and 'believe with all conviction'. In their place went a more natural, relaxed way of reaching their audience. When the Queen made a nationwide broadcast in which she improvised on the prepared speech, the result was seen in the telegrams of congratulation the Canadians sent her. The traditional Christmas broadcast was also shaken up by Her Majesty. It was so stuffy that she found it increasingly painful. Many of her subjects found it embarrassing.

To change the pattern, Elizabeth barred the habitual speech to camera in 1979 when she authorised the making of a full-length documentary film about the life of the Royal Family. The result was the highly acclaimed '*The Royal Family*', which has done much to dispel the 'stiff' public image of the Royals and particularly the Queen herself.

The Queen usually spends autumn at Buckingham Palace, Christmas at Windsor and Sandringham, Easter at Windsor, part of the early summer at Holyroodhouse and summer at Balmoral. Sandringham and Balmoral belong to her personally but the rest are paid for by the Government.

Buckingham Palace is constructed in four wings built round a gravelled quadrangle that the public has not been able to view since the East front, facing the Mall, was built in the time of Victoria and Albert. There is a basement and four floors. The Queen and Prince Philip live in the North wing of the first floor.

Visitors usually stay in suites ranged on either side of the front balcony. The entire wing was furnished from the Brighton Pavilion and reflects the varied taste of George IV, the exotic Prince Regent.

The Palace was the fourth building to be the Seat of Majesty. After palaces at Westminster, Whitehall and St. James's had housed Royal Families for seven hundred years, King George III's consort, Charlotte of Mecklenburg-Strelitz, was given Buckingham Palace as her private home in 1762.

Sir Charles Sheffield, illegitimate son of the Duke of Buckingham, sold Buckingham House to the Crown for £28,000. When King George and Charlotte moved in on May 22, 1762 it became their family home, but they continued to use St. James's Palace for public functions.

Although Buckingham Palace is the envy of millions of tourists and her subjects, it is unpopular with the Queen. She thinks it too large and noisy and much prefers living in Windsor Castle. With typical British understatement, despite their German ancestry, both King George IV and Prince Philip spoke lightly of the Palace.

To George IV it was his *'pied-à-terre',* and when in 1970 the Queen and Philip were greeted on their way back from a trip to Dakar she said: 'It seems odd to be welcomed into one's own house,' he replied, 'This isn't ours – it's a tied cottage.'

TODAY THE Palace, as well as having a post office, includes an office building, a centre of communications, an art gallery open to the public and stables. It is forty times larger than in George III's days when he announced that it should be known as 'The Queen's House'.

The Palace staff is divided into two groups: those who have contact with the Queen – Household – and those who do not. The latter are clerks, officials and serving staff. Members of the Household wear a special evening coat – blue velvet collar and brass buttons stamped with the Royal Cipher.

More than four hundred people work full time to keep the Monarchy functioning at the Palace. The wage bill is around £1,500,000 a year. The three senior members of the Household are the Lord Chamberlain, the Lord Steward and the Master of the Horse. They are responsible respectively for the 'above stairs', 'below stairs' and 'out-of-doors' duties.

In the mid-Nineteenth Century there were demarcation disputes between these Royal servants. Cleaning inside the windows was the duty of the Lord Chamberlain. But cleaning outside was the responsibility of the Commissioner of Woods and Forests. The Lord Steward had to lay the fire but the Lord Chamberlain's department had to light it. Often their Majesties were left freezing.

The Household staff – sometimes called 'All the Queen's Men and Women' – have four things in common. They tend to have titles, they are fond of horses, they are good at their jobs – and the Queen likes them.

The Master of the Household looks after the daily expenditure, including the wages of the staff. The Lord Chamberlain is responsible for all ceremonial duties. He is the senior officer of the Household and wears a golden key on ceremonial occasions to signify his office. He appoints Royal chaplains, Royal physicians, surgeons and other Household officers, superintends the collection of works of art and makes arrangements for garden parties.

The Master of the Horse is the third-ranking officer at Court. He is in charge of the Sovereign's stables and responsible for providing the horses, carriages and cars required for processions and for the daily needs of the Royal Family.

Senior female members of the Household are the ladies-in-waiting. They usually come from a well-bred conservative background, share the Queen's interests, her hobbies, and to some extent her attitudes. The senior lady-in-waiting is the Mistress of the Robes, the most important Court appointment given to a woman. She has charge of the wardrobe and works out a rota for the other ladies-in-waiting. She sees that Her Majesty has everything to hand, acts as a companion and goes to her for a friendly gossip when things get too quiet.

The role of the ladies-in-waiting goes back to the Norman Conquest, when William the Conqueror's Queen, Matilda, crossed the Channel accompanied by a group of ladies. Her Majesty now has a total of eleven officially designated ladies-in-waiting, while the Queen Mother has twelve.

They are in attendance to fetch and carry for her and make all the arrangements necessary to ease her day. They are always a pace away on public occasions, ready to carry the bouquets of flowers or a gift which has been presented to the Queen. They get no pay for their work – just a small clothing allowance and travelling expenses.

It's all done, as one of the Ladies of the Bedchamber once said, for love. 'Those who have the privilege of being appointed lady-in-waiting serve Her Majesty out of love and loyalty.'

Each female member of the Royal Family is entitled to ladies-in-waiting. The Princess of Wales has four, Princess Anne six, Princess Margaret ten, the Duchess of Gloucester four, Princess Alice seven, the Duchess of Kent four and Princess Alexandra four. They are, according to one Palace source, required 'to be present, yet not to be seen; to help but not to be obvious when doing it; to oil the wheels of modern monarchy.'

Two Ladies of the Bedchamber, who are usually peeresses, attend the Queen on provincial tours, charity galas and some State occasions. There are also four Women of the Bedchamber who do the day-to-day work, such as answering correspondence and attending the Queen on less grand occasions. They have an office at the Palace and work between one and three-week rotas. Usually they are daughters of peers and are paid £1,000 a year plus expenses.

Even though the Civil Servants' Union represents nearly two hundred pages, footmen, maids and other Royal servants, they are, in general, modest in their wage demands. When the Queen had a 'pay rise' recently the only observation was from a servant at Windsor Castle. 'There is no likelihood of a rush for pay increases,' he said stiffly. 'We are a pretty dedicated bunch and we like our employer.'

They pay a high price for their dedication, many having to take additional jobs to supplement their income.

But serving the Queen has its compensations 'in kind'. Commented another servant at Windsor. 'Many of them get good accommodation at low prices. There is total security.'

AFTERNOON GARDEN parties at Buckingham Palace were begun by Queen Victoria so that she could meet a wider range of the upper classes. In the early 1960's, however, the occasions became far more democratic. On three Thursday afternoons in July the Lord Chamberlain invites about 9,000 people to tea at the Palace. Each guest costs the Queen about £2.50 and at each party more than £4,000 is spent on bandstands, tents, toilets and ambulance facilities. There are three tents: the Royal, the Diplomatic and the General (for the general public).

The guests mingle on thirty-nine acres of the most extensive lawns in the world. In the rose garden alongside they can see three varieties – 'Queen Elizabeth', 'Silver Lining' and 'Peace' – among the camellias, lilies, delphiniums, rhododendrons and azaleas. Trees range from a black mulberry, whose label proclaims it was 'Planted in 1609 when the Mulberry Garden was formed by James I', to an avenue of Indian chestnuts created in 1961 to screen the garden from skyscrapers.

Investitures are always held in the ballroom. The Throne is set on a dais at the west end where it is surmounted by a huge white arch. On top of this arch are profiles of Queen Victoria and the Prince Consort, supported by figures emblematic of History and Fame. At Investitures the Queen stands before the canopy above the Throne, while those to be honoured by her enter the ballroom through a door on the left.

As part of recent efforts by most of the Royals to understand at first hand what is happening beyond the Palace gates, the Queen now holds monthly lunches for about twelve people. Her guest list is deliberately wide, ranging from pop singers and comedians to ambassadors and visiting statesmen. They have proved to be highly successful, with both Sovereign and subjects getting to know each other better in a semi-formal atmosphere. Recalls one lucky guest; 'She goes out of her way to make you feel at ease, and by the time you've reached the second course you tend to forget that you are in the Palace and begin to let your hair down – not too far down, though.'

For no one can never really let his or her hair down in the presence of the Queen. No matter how friendly she may appear to be, due to her natural politeness and genuine interest in people, it is inbred in her never to forget who she is and what she represents. So over-familiarity is put down – with style, of course! The Royal Family generally counts among its intimates three types of people – relations, overseas regal families and longstanding friends. With these an informal pattern of banter is permitted. With others, however – politicians, visiting statesmen, guests at Buckingham Palace, staff and those fortunate enough to be in a line-up for a smile and handshake – conversation can only go so far. Then a degree of aloofness may be necessary.

When someone is introduced to the Queen, they are briefed beforehand to call her 'Ma'am'. Etiquette is such that one never takes her hand unless it is offered and then the grip must not be too strong – neither must it be too weak. She has a distaste for 'wet fish' handshakes. No one talks to the Queen – she always begins a discussion. People meeting her are warned beforehand that they must not let a brief chat develop into a monologue. This is because her time is usually short so she values a few words with everyone rather than being engaged in chit-chat with just one forceful acquaintance.

When she does stop to have a discussion with someone, the person is often astonished at how much she knows about him or his interests. This is because she is very well served by her staff, who give her a detailed briefing on whom she is likely to meet.

In the Palace the Queen and Prince Philip have what are virtually two large flats on the first floor. Below them are the offices of the principal Royal Officials. On the second floor are bedrooms and bathrooms for members of the family – Prince Andrew, Prince Edward and also for Princess Anne and her husband when they are in London. Anne has grown to dislike London more and more, so when she has an engagement in the capital she only stays at the Palace overnight. She then dashes back to Gatcombe Park, her Cotswold home.

Prince Philip's apartments consist of an office, a small reference and general library in a lobby, bedroom, bathroom and a big dressing-room containing some of his clothes and uniforms.

Among the people the Queen has entertained in her Palace have been President de Gaulle of France, Kosygin of Russia, Yuri Gagarin, the first man to circle the earth from space, Billy Graham, the American evangelist, and Pope John Paul II.

THOSE ATTENDING any of her banquets step into a sugar-plum world where time seems to have stood still... footmen wearing scarlet livery decorated with gold braid, scarlet plush knee-breeches, white stockings and black silver-buckled shoes... They used to powder their hair with wheat flour and very fine rice flour. Heated in a tin in the oven, then mixed with water, it was then plastered on the hair where it dried hard. It looked very fine but was messy and disagreeable and often gave the footmen bad colds. The practice has been stopped since the Coronation on the orders of the Queen.

Until recently, food for State banquets used to arrive at the table almost cold. This was because the banqueting hall is a long way from the kitchens. The problem has now been solved by loading meals in the kitchens on to large, electrically-heated trolleys, which are then put on a service lift to the basement. There the trolleys are pushed through the long corridors to another service lift at the other end of the Palace. They are then wheeled to a small room adjoining the hall, which has hot-plates and other kitchen equipment.

Food at Windsor Castle is still likely to be luke-warm, though. The Castle is so old that service lifts from the kitchens cannot be fitted and the corridors are so full of steps that trolleys cannot be used. The result is that everything has to be carried on trays through a labyrinth of passageways. A footman told me that a measuring instrument was once strapped to his leg to discover how far he walked in one day at Windsor. It turned out to be ten miles.

The dinner service for small gatherings at the Palace is usually Royal Worcester, specially made and presented to the Queen by the Brigade of Guards. It is of the palest ivory within a gold border, each piece bearing the crest of one of the five regiments forming the Brigade.

The Queen's taste in food is essentially straightforward. She likes plain, English-style dishes. She is said to hate oysters, garlic and milk puddings, but enjoys banana caramel with plenty of syrup, and prefers vegetable omelettes to richer meat dishes. Prince Philip is very fond of game, while Prince Charles likes meatballs or goulash, banana sandwiches spread with jam, and bread-and-butter pudding laced with rum.

At State banquets every effort is made to make guests happy. When guests are expected, a footman strides through the corridors swinging a censer of smouldering lavendar to freshen the air. And meticulous attention is paid throughout every operation to get things exactly right.

As Lord Cobbold, the former Lord Chamberlain, said: 'All ceremonial is ridiculous, but people like it and it retains some sort of dignity. As long as it doesn't get out of balance it isn't a bad thing.'

In the 1980s, however, there are striking discords between the medieval and the modern. At a State Banquet, for example, the footmen wear gold-braided scarlet with knee breeches and pink stockings. Members of the Royal Family and guests of honour walk in procession from the Music Room. Just before they reach the Ballroom, the Lord Chamberlain turns to face the Queen and enters backwards in front of her.

A few minutes later there is a characteristic contrast with this touch of ancient ceremony. Concealed in flowers on either side of the Queen at the top of the dining-table are red and green 'traffic lights'. A steward standing behind the Monarch operates these lights so that the footmen, acting as waiters – though they are never called waiters – can be summoned to serve instantly.

When the Queen and Prince Philip make a tour abroad packing is a major operation presided over by a senior official with a group of experienced staff. The trunks are numbered, the contents listed and a loose-leaf file opened to record every detail, including what is to be worn on each day at each function.

Among the mountains of luggage taken on tour are cases of some of the most fabulous jewels. In addition to the State regalia that makes up the famous Crown Jewels kept under guard at the Tower of London, the Queen has an enormous collection of personal trinkets.

The ongoing constitutional duties of monarchy must also be ensured while the Queen is abroad, so three or four senior members of the Royal Family are appointed Councillors of State. Any two of them can exercise many of the powers of the sovereign, including the signing of Acts of Parliament but excluding the awarding of honours.

☆ ☆ ☆ ☆ ☆ ☆

The Queen Today – page 273

PAGEANTRY

Painter Annigoni captured the great beauty of the Queen with this now world famous painting while photographer Baron (right) did an even more formal pause with his camera.

Left, formal portraits of The Queen and Prince Philip at Buckingham Palace and (bottom) The Queen on her way to the State Opening of Parliament. Above – The ceremony of the State Opening.

TROOPING THE COLOUR. Her Majesty's official birthday is always on a Saturday in June . . . It is both a highlight of the British tourist season and a regular fixture in the Queen's year. Certainly the most spectacular of the large number of events the Queen attends. Trooping the Colour always draws huge crowds. These are some of the scenes (and previous pages) that make the ceremony such a fascinating spectacle.

The balcony of Buckingham Palace is one big happy family scene

as the young Royal children watch the fly-past of the Royal Air Force.

The Queen (left) inspects the Yeomen of the Guard in the gardens of Buckingham Palace and (above) makes an inspection of her own Company of Archers in Scotland. Overleaf, The Queen and Prince Philip, both wearing the robes of the insignia of The British Empire, of which she is the Monarch, leave St Paul's Cathedral after a service for the Order.

Dating from 1349, "The Most Noble and Amiable Company of St. George named the Garter" is the oldest order of Christian chivalry in Britain. Originally the order comprised only twenty-five Knights, but this number was increased in 1831 to allow the Prince of Wales and other members of the British and foreign Royal Families to be admitted. The Garter Ceremony at which new Knights are invested, takes place at Windsor Castle, following which the Knights of the Order walk to St. George's Chapel, preceded by the Military Knights of Windsor and various heralds. A service is then held in the chapel, after which the Queen and her family return in open carriages to the castle. The colourful ceremony takes place in a beautiful and historic location. There is little wonder, therefore, that it attracts large crowds.

This charming picture of mother and daughters was taken by Norman Parkinson

to commemorate Her Majesty Queen Elizabeth The Queen Mother's 80th birthday.

St. Paul's Cathedral was the majestic setting for the colourful spectacle of the Thanksgiving Service for the Queen Mother's eightieth birthday, attended by all her family and friends (and overleaf).

SILVER JUBILEE YEAR. The Gold State Coach, pulled by eight Windsor Greys, leaves

Buckingham Palace with the Queen and Prince Philip en route for St. Paul's Cathedral.

The Gold State Coach, with the Queen and Prince Philip, makes its way down Fleet Street

on the way to St. Paul's Cathedral for the Silver Jubilee Thanksgiving Serivce.

The Thanksgiving Service for Queen Elizabeth II's Silver Jubilee in St. Paul's Cathedral (and overleaf).

PRINCE CHARLES' WEDDING

The Royal Carriages make their way to St. Paul's Cathedral for the Wedding of The Prince of Wales to Lady Diana Spencer. Overleaf: the bride's carriage on its way to St. Paul's.

Sports

Proud father the Earl of Spencer escorts his youngest daughter, Lady Diana, down the aisle of St. Paul's Cathedral.

The Queen, Prince Philip and other members of the Royal Family watch lovingly as their first

son is married and (overleaf) Prince Charles slips the wedding ring on Princess Diana's finger.

The Wedding ceremony of The Prince of Wales to Lady Diana Spencer in St. Paul's Cathedral on 29 July 1981 (above and next five pages).

The triumphant return of the Bride and Groom to Buckingham Palace.

Before her first appearance on the balcony of Buckingham Palace, Princess

Diana, under the watchful eye of the Queen, checks her bridesmaids' dresses.

Above, The Prince of Wales kisses The Princess of Wales' hand and (right) more jubilant scenes on the balcony. Overleaf, history was created when, after asking The Queen's permission, the Prince of Wales kisses his bride in public – to the delight of the crowds.

The Royal group photographed by Lord Patrick Lichfield at Buckingham Palace.

Prince Charles and Princess Diana with Prince Andrew and Prince Edward, and

the Page and Maids of Honour. Overleaf, a bow from Prince Charles to his wife.

ROYAL TOURS

Pageantry of a different kind when The Queen, Prince Philip, Princess Anne, Captain Mark Phillips and the late Earl of Mountbatten were greeted in Goroka, Papua New Guinea by some of Her majesty's most loyal Commonwealth subjects, the fierce warriors known as "The Mudmen". Overleaf, more Papuan tribesmen

Her Majesty The Queen and Prince Philip are welcomed by King Taufa'ahau Tupou IV and the Queen of Tonga.

Overleaf, The Queen is dwarfed by the 28-stone King as she pauses in the gardens of the Royal Palace, and (below left) looks amazed by the fare.

Queen of New Zealand and Queen of the Maoris. Right, the Queen received the traditional Maori challenge during two separate visits to New Zealand and, overleaf, opens the new session of the New Zealand Parliament in Wellington.

The Cook islanders provided an original mode of transportation when warriors

carried the Queen, Princess Anne and Captain Mark Phillips on their shoulders.

Queen of Mexico – Her Majesty dazzles her hosts with this beautiful green evening dress and tiara and (overleaf) The Queen and Prince Philip were acclaimed by more than two million Mexicans who gave them a tickertape welcome in Mexico City.

The British Solomon Islands provided another colourful welcome for the Queen who is wearing a plastic covering over her shoes to protect them from the dust and mud.

AB

Her Majesty The Queen, wearing a long navy blue dress and matching hat is welcomed at Riyad Airport by King Khaled of Saudi Arabia and his family. Overleaf, The Queen and King Khaled before dinner in an Arab tent.

British fashion could never hope for a better ambassador, as the Queen showed in Saudi Arabia.

XS793
EIIR

The Queen was welcomed by a thousand dancers in Malawi...a welcome which also marked Prince Andrew's first Royal Tour.

The Queen, greeted by the islanders as "Mrs. Gwin", and Prince Philip go ashore at Tuvalu, one of the smallest Commonwealth islands in the Pacific. Previous pages, the Queen's canoe being carried by natives in Tuvalu. Above, the Queen borne ashore in a native canoe, and (Top Left and opposite) the Queen, ready to take holiday snapshots, and Prince Philip enjoy the festivities.

The Queen with Mrs. Indira Gandhi during her 1983 visit to India.

Prince William who made his first Royal Tour in Australia, and (right) New Zealand at the grand age of one, pictured with his parents, Prince Charles and Princess Diana.

Britannia becomes more than a floating palace during Royal tours; it serves as an office and nerve centre of Monarchy and heads of State. Other luggage (overleaf) which includes specially selected items from her wardrobe, and jewellery for receptions. The Queen's luggage is carried

dignitaries as well as British businessmen can be entertained on board. To set up temporary residence the Queen requires just over seven tons of in huge mauve trunks with her name printed on each one. Prince Philip's luggage is carried in separate trunks, as are the State papers.

H·M·YACHT
FROM ROYAL SCOTTISH MUSEUM
CHAMBERS STREET
EDINBURGH

COMPTROLLER
OFFICE
K

Back in England, it is life as usual at Buckingham Palace with Prince Philip . . . and a stroll by the lake with the corgis.

FIRST

The Royal Landau, drawn by the Windsor greys, arrives in the unsaddling enclosure.

Her Majesty shows her happiness among the elegant crowd at Ascot.

The Queen with the Queen Mother and Princess Diana at Ascot, and (right) the carriage drive to Ascot with Prince Philip.

This happy family group was recorded for the baptism of Zara Phillips, second child of Princess Anne and Captain Mark Phillips, in the Music Room at Buckingham Palace, 1981. Right, the scene after Princess Anne's own christening on 21st October 1950 photographed in the White Drawing Room at Buckingham Palace.

ABC

ABC

An early wave from Prince William posing with his parents in the gardens of their Royal home at Kensington Palace, 1983.

Prince Henry was supposed to be the star at his christening but Prince William was determined to steal the show. The godparents were Lady Sarah Armstrong-Jones, artist Bryan Organ, Gerald Ward (standing left), Carolyn Bartholomew and Lady Susan Hussey (standing right).

Traditional ties between the United States and Great Britain are always revived and made firmer when the Queen and the President meet. On the
they rode together (above) in Windsor Great Park. The

previous page President Reagan and Her Majesty are seen during his last official visit mounted up in the stables at Windsor Castle. Afterwards Queen was on 'Burmese', one of her favourite horses.

Her Majesty the Queen and Prince Philip being received by His Holiness Pope John Paul II at the Vatican.

Prince Charles and Princess Diana with Prince William and infant Prince Henry during their Scottish holidays in 1985.

Prince Charles with Prince William and Publisher Robert Maxwell, 1985.

THE QUEEN TODAY

SPARKLING MONARCH

THE CROWN JEWELS belong to the Sovereign and are at the disposal of her consort, but are not a personal possession. It is a large collection, varying from fabulously valuable and historic jewels to a quantity of pieces of only sentimental importance, such as mourning rings for forgotten royal dukes and princes of the Eighteenth and Nineteenth Centuries. Many of them have been inherited from past sovereigns. Queen Mary left her the greatest amount, but throughout her reign the Queen has received countless birthday presents, wedding gifts, gifts from corporations and countries.

She inherited her most valuable brooch from Queen Mary – a pear-shaped diamond of 92 carats and a square diamond of 62 carats, which are the third and fourth parts of the Cullinan Diamond.

The Cullinan was the largest gem diamond crystal ever discovered in the world. It weighed 3,025 carats, about one pound and a half, and was found at the Premier Mine three hundred miles north-east of Kimberley in 1905. It was named after Sir Thomas Cullinan, Chairman of the Premier Diamond Company. The rough diamond was bought by the Transvaal Government in 1907 for presentation to King Edward VII on his sixty-sixth birthday, and marked the reconciliation between the Afrikaaners and Britain after the Boer War.

The Queen's first tiara was a wedding gift from Queen Mary. It had been a wedding present in 1983 to Queen Mary herself from the girls of Great Britain and Ireland. The diamond tiara is a particular favourite of the Queen's because it is very light in weight and delicate in appearance.

'My best diamonds' was her description of twenty-one diamonds given to her as a twenty-first birthday present from the Government of South Africa. These diamonds were cut and polished in Johannesburg and varied in size up to ten carats. They were presented to the Princess to set as a necklace. Later it was shortened and the remaining diamonds were mounted into a matching bracelet.

Her engagement ring is a solitaire diamond supported by diamond shoulders, the stones being heirlooms belonging to Prince Philip's mother.

A gift from Queen Mary, at the time of her engagement, was a brooch consisting of a large diamond bow, originally presented to her on her own marriage in 1893 by the County of Dorset. Queen Mary also gave her grand-daughter earrings consisting of one large pearl and a small diamond, which were originally a wedding gift to Queen Mary from the County of Devon.

Other items of jewellery included the world's finest rose-pink diamond. The donor, Dr. John T. Williamson, was a solitary Canadian geologist who founded his own mine in 1940 in what was then called Tanganyika. He made a gift to her of this diamond weighing 54 carats in the rough. It was delicately cut to 23.6 carats but for many years the Queen was undecided how to have it set. She eventually opted for a brooch six years later at the time of her Coronation. The diamond is at the centre of a flower spray brooch, jonquil shaped with curved petals and navette-cut diamonds, one on each side of the stalk to represent leaves. It measures 4½ inches.

When she became Queen, Elizabeth inherited all the beautiful pieces of Crown Jewellery. Foremost amongst the personal jewellery passed from sovereign to sovereign is the Diamond Diadem, which Her Majesty wore on her way to her Coronation and wears whilst driving each year in the Irish State Coach for the State Opening of Parliament.

A necklace from the Crown Jewellery collection which the Queen is particularly fond of and wore at her Coronation is the diamond collet necklace with a drop-shaped diamond suspended from the centre collet. It was orinally made for Queen Victoria from twenty-eight brilliant collets, of which the nine largest stones weighed between 11¼ and 8¼ carats.

Among her brooches is a spray of 150 diamonds, presented by the Commonwealth of Australia to the Queen during her State Visit to Canberra in 1954. It measures four inches and was designed and made in Australia. She has usually worn the spray on return visits to Australia.

A diamond fern brooch, the New Zealand emblem, was given to the Queen by the women of Auckland on Christmas Day 1953 and this is also worn by the Queen on return visits there.

WIFE AND MOTHER

AMID ALL THE other demands on her time, the Queen has always managed to fulfil what to her is still the most important role in her life – being a wife and mother. She has helped her children through all the usual growing pains of youth and those moments of bewilderment with life. Her encouragement is always there whenever one of them thinks the going is getting too tough.

Elizabeth, remembering the warm, loving atmosphere of her own childhood, never went back on the arrangement she made with herself that there would be no barriers between her and the children; no governesses or nannies stealing all their love. Nursery staff were employed – but mother and father were the people the children usually saw first thing in the morning and last thing at night. As toddlers, the children would snuggle up next to her on a couch to listen to a story. The most popular ones were *'Tales of Beatrix Potter'*; the adventures of *'Baba the Elephant'* and *'Tin-Tin'*.

They were all capable of pranks and mischief, however. Charles used to race round the corridors of Buckingham Palace with his friends, play risky games of hide-and-seek on the roof of Windsor Castle, or slip a piece of ice down the collar of a footman – for which he would get a spanking.

To teach them the value of money, pocket money was doled out in small sums. Although Prince Andrew was entitled to an income of more than £17,000 a year when he was eighteen, the Queen insisted he should not be handed this amount. It was kept in trust for him and he was given a small allowance each week.

As well as training them for their lives as Royals, the Queen and Prince Philip have passed on to them their own habits of not being extravagant with money. Watching the pennies with the Queen once went as far as ordering the Royal Stables to use old shredded newspapers to provide bedding for horses – considerably cheaper than straw!

Heating and lighting bills are kept to a minimum. The Queen often walks round Buckingham Palace at night switching off extra lights. At Sandringham and Balmoral, visitors are advised to put on extra sweaters because the radiators are strictly off in the day. Her Majesty is well known as a saver of odd bits of string. She has been seen to pop them in her pocket rather than throw them away.

She rarely carries money. Coins and notes, when needed, are proffered by a lady-in-waiting, equerry or detective. The Queen sometimes buys things on credit. She was once sent a letter by a credit company accusing her of falling behind on payments for a tractor bought for the Windsor estate. The letter, addressed to Mrs. Elizabeth Regina, turned out to be 'computer error'. But it revealed that Her Majesty does use hire purchase.

At home, Elizabeth and Philip are just ordinary parents to their children – a mother and father they can turn to for advice and help. When any of the Royal Family refers to the Queen in public, however, it is always on very formal basis. She is never called 'my mother' in a speech – always 'the Queen', although Prince Philip is frequently called 'my father'.

Charles has said of his father's influence on his education: 'His attitude was very simple. He told me what were the pros and cons. Of all the possibilities and attractions he told me what he thought best. Because I had come to see how wise he was, by the time I had to be educated I had perfect confidence in my father's judgment. When children are young you have to decide for them. How can they decide for themselves?'

Throughout the childhood of all her children there were always requests for the young Princess and Princes to appear in public. The Queen resisted them all, no matter how worthy the cause – she remembered when she was thrust into the public arena as a young Princess. She insisted that they should have a normal childhood, as far as was possible. To her they were, above everything else, children; so the Queen protected them and nurtured them to the stage when they could be made aware of their Stately duties.

Elizabeth had always hoped, of course, that she would never have to take the Throne so soon after marriage. She had wanted to go through the experience of being the wife of a Naval officer, a mother and home-builder before accepting the duties of the Crown.

Taking on these duties so early in life, depriving her of so much of the freedom that others in their twenties could expect, has influenced the Queen's attitude towards Prince Charles. She knows what it is like to have to bear so early the monarchial chains of office. For this reason she wants Charles to lead an undisturbed domestic life before it is his turn to take over the Throne.

Prince Charles frequently says that it could be thirty years before he becomes King, pointing out how healthy and keen for the job his mother still is. Waiting for so long would mean Charles being well in his sixties before he has the chance to rule. The Queen and her advisers would, nevertheless, like the Heir to the Throne to still be young and full of vigour when his time to don the kingly mantle arrives. Should the Queen, as some people say, decide to abdicate in favour of her son, it will certainly not be until he has had a better chance than she had of being a parent first and a monarch second. Talk of abdication is always strongly denied by Buckingham Palace. In any case, 'abdication' is a dirty word among a family that remembers how King Edward VIII's departure affected them.

Elizabeth helped Charles through all the usual growing pains of youth. Her encouragement was always there. When he first went away to school she wrote to him almost daily, feeding him family gossip to keep up his spirits.

At university Charles occasionally found the task a struggle, and felt lonely. The Queen would visit him privately in his rooms at Trinity College, Cambridge, where they would talk over his problems while he prepared a simple meal for the two of them.

The Queen attended to her son's upbringing with a typical mother's gentleness; Prince Philip provided a grittier influence.

CHARLES AND PHILIP have a very close relationship, based on love and respect for one another's achievements. Their personalities differ considerably: Prince Philip has always been the more abrasive, while Charles has more gentleness of spirit. As one of the Duke's friends once said... 'Charles is not a bit like him.'

At first Charles seemed to try hard to emulate his father. He was tempted to adopt Philip's occasional high-handed style. But as he grew out of his teens the Prince developed a likeable personality of his own, while his father began to mellow.

Charles was taught nearly all his physical skills by his father, and in this way they grew closer. Philip would take him out in bitter wintry weather among the heather around Balmoral to teach him to shoot. Charles bagged his first grouse when he was ten. Philip showed his son how to fish, and at home he would spend an hour after tea teaching him to swim in the Palace pool. Charles could swim a length before he was five years old, and is now an excellent swimmer.

Father and son would occasionally have a boisterous game of football in the Palace grounds, with the corgis barking round their heels. Sometimes the Queen and toddler Anne joined in the fun. The Prince was determined that his son would not have a pampered, soft life. He once noticed a servant leaping to close a door that schoolboy Charles had failed to shut. 'Leave it alone, man,' he shouted. 'He's got hands. He can go back and do it himself.'

Prince Philip's greatest influence in the early days was in bringing the Royal educational style into the Twentieth Century. He made sure that the boys learned how to be independent as soon as possible, packing them off to boarding-schools where they had to stand on their own feet from the age of nine or ten. Anne, too, left the shelter of home at thirteen to become a boarder at fashionable Benenden in Kent.

The boys, at their father's instigation, were to face a tougher educational regime when they reached thirteen. Philip sent them to his old *alma-mater*, Gordonstoun. He had been subjected to its harsh, cold-shower system and had thought it had done him the world of good. Why wouldn't it have the same results with his own sons?

Gordonstoun was to be an institution that Andrew – who has inherited his father's ways – found easier to accept. Charles and Edward were more sensitive than the middle brother. Charles has especially unhappy memories of Gordonstoun, which is mainly a collection of crude huts. Dormitories have unpainted wooden walls, bare floors and uncomfortable iron beds. An obligatory cold shower has to be taken every morning, no matter what the weather. The school motto, *'Plus est en vous'* ('There is more in you') heralds a harsh system aimed at stretching to the fullest both physical and intellectual capabilities. That, at least, is the idea.

Thanks to Elizabeth, all the Royal sons and daughter are great home-lovers. As a group they are closer to each other and their near relations than many families these days. Their happiest moments are when they are together. Whether at Buckingham Palace or one of the other Royal homes, they are a tight little group that finds a welcome relief from the pressures around them. When the cheers and flagwaving have ended, they still have each other.

They value one another and protect one another. If any of them is abroad, they keep in constant touch by telephone or letter. None of them does anything without discussing it first with the others. During the break-up of her marriage, Princess Margaret was helped through the trauma by her family. The Queen and Prince Philip took a sympathetic interest in what was happening, not merely because of a constitutional responsibility but because they wished to offer family comfort.

Their concern has also extended to Lord Snowdon and the couple's children, Viscount

Linley and Lady Sarah Armstrong-Jones. Lord Snowdon is still in close touch with the family at the end of the Mall and especially with the Queen Mother, despite the divorce.

The Queen best summed up her attitude towards family life when she said at the time of her Silver Wedding Anniversary: 'A marriage begins by joining man and wife together, but this relationship between two people, however deep at the time, needs to develop and mature with the passing years. For that it must be held firm in the web of the family relationships, between parents and children, between grandparents and grandchildren, between cousins, aunts and uncles. If I am asked today what I think about family life after twenty-five years of marriage, I can answer with simplicity and conviction. I am for it.'

The late King George VI once observed: 'We are not a family – we are "a firm".' Walter Bagehot, the Victorian expert on the Monarchy, still preferred to regard the folks at Buckingham Palace as being 'a family on a Throne'. He commented in 1867; 'It brings down the pride of sovereignty to the level of petty life.' Most people must surely be happier to look upon the Queen as head of a family rather than a corporation. A long-serving member of the Royal Household once told me: 'I never feel as if I'm working at Buckingham Palace – it's like being part of a very busy family.'

A family, but certainly one with a rare existence. Their lives are their work. 'They do on-the-job training, so to speak,' according to Prince Philip, 'and learn the trade or business or craft just from being with us and watching us function and seeing the whole organisation around us. They can't avoid it. What is much more difficult is bringing them up as people.'

Bringing up such a family, under the world's spotlight, is one of the major accomplishments of Her Majesty and her Consort. Charles, Anne, Andrew and Edward have always enjoyed that happy family life. Now two of them have children of their own, and Andrew and Edward are beginning to lead more independent lives.

The Queen and Prince Charles have much in common. He takes after her in his kindness and gentle qualities. She does not like change and Charles has the same conservative attitude. They are both aware of the continuing constitutional roles they shoulder. They sense that they not only belong to the nation and Commonwealth but are also the ongoing link of this heritage.

In a recent BBC interview with broadcaster John Dunn, Charles was asked: 'Do you have a great sense of history and destiny about being King Charles III?' The Prince answered: 'No, I don't think so at all. It's always a dangerous thing, isn't it, to feel sometimes that you have a destiny. A lot of people throughout history have felt they had destinies and they've done an awful lot of damage...

'Who knows what the future will hold? I believe in *now*, getting on from day to day with the things that I feel strongly about and the things that I feel need pursuing in this country. That's the only thing I can do. I could fall under a bus tomorrow, couldn't I? And I think it would be awful pity just to think about what might come in years ahead. I would have wasted a whole lot of time; there's an awful lot that needs doing in this country.'

A ROYAL WEDDING

WHILE WAITING to see what the future held for him, Charles made one of the most important decisions about the future of the Monarchy when he chose not only a bride but a future queen. Lady Diana Spencer, now the Princess of Wales, was welcomed into the family as the perfect choice for a future Queen of England. The Queen is said to be delighted with her. The Princess says, 'I have the best mother-in-law in the world.'

The age of the arranged marriage had passed by the time Charles wanted to marry a woman he truly loved. There were still some restrictions as to his choice, though. George III's Royal Marriage Act of 1772 meant that Charles, as Heir in direct line to George II, was in the hands of his mother and of Parliament when it came to picking a bride. He had to satisfy the requirements of the Queen, the House of Lords and the House of Commons. Until the age of twenty-five he could only marry with the consent of the Queen. If she had refused permission, he could still ask for the approval of both Houses of Parliament. Had the Queen turned down his choice, it seemed highly unlikely that, even in this democratic age, the Lords and the Commons would approve of the match if the girl was so eminently unsuitable as to be formally rejected by Her Majesty.

Diana's credentials were impeccable. She was born at Park House in Norfolk, just a stone's throw from Sandringham. Her illustrious lineage stretched back to the reign of Charles II in 1630. Her family were distantly related to the Royal Family and her father, Edward, the eighth Earl of Spencer, was a very close friend of the Queen and Prince Philip.

The Spencer children used to play with the Royal youngsters. Diana's grandmother, Ruth, Lady Fermoy, was not only a close friend of the Queen Mother but one of her ladies-in-waiting. So when, at the age of 32, Charles announced his engagement to Diana, the nineteen-year-old kindergarten teacher was given a warm welcome into the Royal household.

When they married on July 29, 1981, they broke traditions from the start with their choice of where they wanted the ceremony to take place – St. Paul's Cathedral, which has a reputation of being 'less stuffy' than Westminster Abbey, the scene of Coronations and Royal Marriages for centuries.

There were changes, too, on the vows Diana would make. She was to vow to love and honour but not to obey Prince Charles. The decision, made by the couple after talks with the Archbishop of Canterbury, upset traditionalists in the Church. For 'obey' was used by the Queen in her marriage in 1947, by Princess Margaret in 1960 and by Princess Anne in 1973.

It was agreed that the bride would be asked: 'Wilt thou love him, comfort him, honour and keep him?' Again the traditionalists were upset, but the Dean of Westminster, Dr Edward Carpenter, came to Diana's aid when he commented: 'I think marriage is the kind of relation where there should be two equal partners, and if there is going to be a dominant partner, it won't be settled by this oath. I think this is much more Christian.'

Two days before the ceremony the Queen gave the future King and his bride a lively ball at Buckingham palace, featuring not only a formal orchestra for waltzes but a jazz band and a pop group, Hot Chocolate, for jiving and rocking. After a dinner for ninety, the cream of the Royal Wedding guests were let loose beneath the brilliant chandeliers of the Investiture Room. The jazzmen and pop group were at one end of the great salon. At the opposite end, the band of the Welsh Guards, complete with platoons of violins, played more sedate waltzes in which the Queen joined with great delight. When the noise grew too loud for the Queen's table, a quick button-press on her 'magic box' – a contraption for controlling the overall volume – reduced the sound.

The next day the Prince of Wales spent his final evening as a bachelor with his mother and father, enjoying one of Britain's biggest firework displays. Before watching two and a half tons of explosives erupt above his head in the skies over Hyde Park, he set light to the first beacon in a nationwide chain of 101 bonfires in front of a crowd estimated at half a million, and before millions of television viewers in Britain, the United States, Canada and Australia. Lady Diana was not present. She was in Clarence House with Queen Elizabeth the Queen Mother, from where she was to set out for the ceremony at St. Paul's.

A million cheering people crammed the streets and office and hotel windows on the three mile route to the Cathedral. The wedding was watched on British television by 39 million viewers and around the world, in seventy-four countries, by 750 million: the largest viewing audience in the entire history of television.

Diana was driven to the ceremony in a 'fairy princess' glass coach pulled by white horses. As she left Clarence House the world was able to get its first glimpse of the dress, designed by David and Elizabeth Emanuel: it was a gown of ivory silk taffeta, finished with frills, bows, lace and a detachable train twenty-five feet long. Breathtaking. It moved famous *Daily Express* columnist, Jean Rook, to write: 'The bride was one great ivory cream thrill with a bouquet like a dripping cool waterfall.'

Diana, riding in the glass coach, sat almost hidden in her spectacular wedding creation of ivory taffeta and old lace. Only when she stepped from the coach on the arm of her father at the Cathedral steps was its true magnificence revealed. Standing behind her were Princess Margaret's daughter, seventeen-year-old Lady Sarah Armstrong-Jones, the chief bridesmaid, four younger bridesmaids and two pages – all were needed to hold that enormous silken train.

Charles did not have a best man but instead was flanked by two Royal 'supporters', his younger brothers, Prince Andrew and Prince Edward.

Bells throughout the entire country rang as Charles and new new Princess walked out of the Cathedral after the ceremony. Salutes of guns could be heard booming round the capital as they travelled to Buckingham Palacethrough the tumultuous streets of London. Back at the Palace, the Royal Couple stepped on to the balcony to greet the millions of well-wishers all over the world.

'Kiss her,' demanded the crowd. The Prince of Wales turned to his bride and whispered, 'Will you kiss me?'. The couple embraced before the cheering crowd. It was the first kiss ever seen on the balcony of Buckingham Palace and the Prince observed protocol by turning to his mother and asking 'Is it all right to kiss?'. The Queen smiled and gave a nod of approval, saying, 'Yes, of course.'

It was the most wildly applauded kiss in the history of British Royalty. For good measure, Charles planted another on Diana's hand. When the Prince led his bride out for the third or fourth time in response to the clamour below, the Queen and Prince Philip deliberately used the side doors of the French windows so as not to draw attention away from the couple.

There were 180 guests, helpers, staff and servants in the grand Ballroom for the Royal Wedding Breakfast. Prince Edward and Prince Andrew announced the arrival of each guest as the Queen was busy clicking away with her gold Rollei camera...'One King of Norway,' Prince Andrew declared – and in came King Olaf. 'One King in Exile' – King Constantine of Greece. The Princes shook rattles, the sort used by football fans, as each guest came through the door.

The grandest Royal Wedding of the age turned 'Lady Di' into the Princess of Wales. Five years after her arrival in the Royal Family, they find it hard to remember how they ever got on without her. Shortly after their marriage, the new Princess was 'launched' into the first of the arduous tours that are more and more a part of her life. There was a six-week trip to Australia and New Zealand, part of the business of 'showing her off' to the Commonwealth.

The first Christmas with the entire family at Windsor proved to be a very special one for the newlyweds. In the middle of the festivities, Charles and Diana let out of the bag the news that the Queen had been waiting for. 'Yes, it's true, Ma'am, I'm pregnant,' she told Her Majesty. The revelation in private was followed soon after by a public announcement.

UNTIL PRINCESS Anne changed the pattern, Royal babies were born at Buckingham Palace. Diana's sister-in-law decided to go into the private wing of a public hospital to have her first child, Peter, nine years ago. Since then, the Lindo Wing of St. Mary's Hospital, Paddington, in one of London's less fashionable districts, has become the regal birthplace...mainly because of the expertise on hand among the country's finest obstetricians.

So it was to St. Mary's Diana went to have the Queen's third grandchild. At the time the Falklands crisis was at its height, and the birth of a new Prince brought happier news to the nation. Prince William made his debut at 9.30 p.m. on June 21 1982 – the longest day of the year.

Prince Charles and Diana waited forty-four days before christening the new Second-in-Line to the Throne. They chose August 4 at Buckingham Palace, the Queen Mother's eighty-second birthday. The names were William Arthur Philip Louis, the last in rememberance of the late Lord Mountbatten.

Eighteen months later on February 14, 1984, Buckingham Palace announced that the Queen was to be a grandmother for the fourth time. She and the Duke of Edinburgh were quoted as being 'absolutely delighted'. The Princess of Wales' second child was born on the morning of Saturday, September 13, 1984, again in the Lindo Wing.

The baby was christened Henry Charles Albert David. Henry has been the name of eight British Kings. The last member of the Royal Family so named was Henry, Duke of Gloucester, one of the Queen's uncles, who died in 1974. Charles derives both from the baby's father and Diana's brother, Viscount Althorp. Albert recalls Queen Victoria's consort and the baby's great-grandfather, who reigned as George VI. David honours the Queen Mother's brother, the late Sir David Bowes-Lyon. A Palace spokesman said, however, that 'he will be known as Harry.'

Elizabeth had, by the time that William and Henry came on the scene, become very familiar with the joys of being a grandma – thanks to Princess Anne's children. The Queen Mother is reputed to have been responsible for bringing Princess Anne and Captain Mark Phillips together, though their paths had previously crossed at a horse trial. She had accepted an invitation to a cellar party in the City of London in honour of the British equestrian team who had returned from the 1968 Mexico Olympic Games with a Gold Medal. The Queen Mother took her grand-daughter along with her.

Captain Phillips, then a lieutenant in a cavalry regiment, was the youngest ever reserve rider with the team and he was obviously greatly attracted to the Princess. She was eighteen and he was twenty. Their great common interest was horses, but they were also drawn to each other as individuals.

Five years later, on November 14, 1973, after the Princess had successfully followed her own riding career, they were married. To commemorate the occasion, the Queen asked her Poet Laureate, Sir John Betjeman, to produce some suitable lines...

'Hundreds of birds in the air
And millions of leaves on the pavement.
Then the bells pealing on
Over Palace and people outside,
All for the words 'I will'
To love's most holy enslavement –
What can we do but rejoice
With a triumphing bridegroom and bride

Her Majesty's first grandson, Master Peter Philips, was born in 1977, and four years later her first grand-daughter, Miss Zara Elizabeth Philips, arrived. The odd first name is a version of a Greek Biblical meaning 'bright as dawn.'

When Princess Anne was nine and Prince Charles eleven, the Queen presented them with a baby brother: Andrew Albert Christian Edward. The Queen had always wanted more than two children, after her Coronation, she had been too busy to take time off for child-bearing.

The Queen's third pregnancy, suspected in June 1959 and known to the family by early July, was intended to be kept secret until after a six-week tour of Canada which she was to complete with Prince Philip that month. That was an achievement in itself.

In the first week of the visit she began to suffer from morning sickness, and consquently it was not long before the Press in Canada began to notice, and its British counterparts to question. Then, as the Queen was obliged to thin out her engagements, the speculation really began.

It seemed unlikely that, after a nine-year gap, the Queen might become a mother again. Therefore, the rumour was confined to pure speculation – sinus trouble, exhaustion, diet – even a touch of the collywobbles. Then, a week after her return to Britain, the announcement was made.

Andrew was the first child born to a Reigning Monarch since the birth of Beatrice to Queen Victoria, 103 years earlier. He showed signs of his dashing personality as an adult from the outset. He was a lively and mischievous little boy. Nothing pleased him more than to tie together the laces on the boots of Palace guardsmen or to put 'whoopee cushions' among his parents' armchairs. 'Not always a little ray of sunshine,' the Queen said drily.

He fitted in with his father's plans for a robust upbringing easier than Charles. One of the results was an eagerness for a Service career. He became a Naval helicopter pilot. As such, he went with his ship to fight for the liberation of the Falkland Islands. The summer of 1982 gave the Queen many anxious days. She shared the worries of other mothers with sons in the fighting zone for Andrew was taking the same risks as the rest of the pilots.

His eventual safe homecoming on the aircraft carrier, *Invincible*, was the focal point of a whole day of family celebrations. Shortly afterwards he was promoted from second to first pilot, qualified after four hundred flying hours to captain his own helicopter – two hundred of those hours had been flown during the Falklands Campaign.

Prince Edward, born in 1964, has the reputation of being the most academically inclined and sensitive of the Queen's children. He has already begun the obligatory Princely years of serving in one of the armed forces – in his case the Royal Marines. Whether or not he makes a career as a shipborne soldier still has to be decided.

IT WAS the stuff of fairytales! The Queen in a golden coach pulled by six white horses, and Prince Charles in a dashing uniform riding behind her in triumphal procession among cheering masses. This happened in London on a memorable June 7, 1977 as part of the Silver Jubilee celebrations marking the twenty-fifth anniversary of the Queen's Accession to the Throne.

The Queen, with the Duke of Edinburgh sitting alongside her, waved to the crowds through the windows of the 216-year-old Golden State Coach. Riding just behind the right wheel was Prince Charles on a sleek black horse given to him by the Royal Canadian Mounted Police – 'The Mounties'. With a silver sword at his side, he was dressed in the tall bearskin and crimson jacket of a colonel in the Welsh Guards. Across his chest was a lavish display of decorations.

The Queen and her family and friends gathered that day in St. Paul's Cathedral for a service of thanksgiving to mark the anniversary. Afterwards she and Prince Philip walked among the crowds in the City of London.

Despite the odd sniping from some quarters, the Jubilee proved that the Royal Family was as popular as ever. The Queen must be one of the best-loved monarchs in the history of the Crown. The feelings of her subjects were well summed up that day by a group of long-haired teenagers, looking more typical of rebellious youth than Royalists, who held up a banner as she passed them on her 'walk-about' in the City of London. It proclaimed: 'Liz Rules, OK'.

The Jubilee was also celebrated with a gruelling tour of the United Kingdom, reaching its climax in a closely guarded visit to Ulster. When the Queen was whirled off the deck of the Royal Yacht *Britannia* by helicopter on her arrival in Belfast, she neared the end of the most monumental monarchial marathon ever undertaken by a British sovereign. Looking back, this was her life during the long days of that tour:

She travelled 7,100 miles by land, sea and air – roughly divided into 1,600 miles on the Royal Train, 1,400 miles aboard *Britannia*, 2,400 miles in one or other of the four Rolls-Royces in constant attendance from the Royal Mews, and a further 1,700 miles in any of the three Andovers and two Wessex helicopters comprising the Queen's Flight.

She was involved in 800 events, illustrating every aspect of national life, and averaging twelve hours a day of stop-watched timing in all twelve regions of Britain. In Scotland the Queen travelled more than 500 miles, during which 1,000 people were formally presented to her in the eleven days she spent North of the border.

In Wales, she travelled about 1,000 miles through seven of the eight counties in three days, shaking hands with 700 people. At the Spithead Review she inspected 100 British warships, 30 foreign warships and 50 auxiliary and merchant craft, In West Germany the Queen reviewed 3,000 British troops and 573 armoured vehicles at Sennelager. Back in Britain in the Eastern Region, she drove through Norfolk and Suffolk, during which she met around 500 people before joining *Britannia* at Felixstowe. Roundly speaking, the Queen shook 5,000 hands and got through an average of four pairs of gloves a day in the process.

On one particularly heavy day, following a train-borne night in an anonymous siding with only the crunch of patrolling guards on the track below to soothe her, the Queen had 41 highly-synchronised items on her rigorously regulated itinerary. Over 5000 handshakes. During the tour she also unveiled 31 commemorative plaques, planted four memorial trees, attended one cricket match and a game of soccer.

In keeping with her wish for a certain degree of economy to temper the Jubilee celebrations, the Queen did not order a special wardrobe from her three couturiers.

Nor did she put on weight, despite sitting through 23 formal luncheons and 13 dinners, and raising her glass in response to interminable toasts, including acknowledgements to seemingly endless addresses of welcome.

THE WORKLOAD ON the Queen has grown enormously since she came to the Throne, and today her duties and responsibilities fall into four main categories. First, there is the work arising from the normal operation of government in the form of information which she receives from Ministers at home and from representatives abroad and submissions which she has to approve and sign. The Queen receives copies of all-important Government papers – reports from foreign ambassadors and Ministers abroad and instructions for replies from the Foreign Office, minutes of Cabinet meetings and minutes of all important conferences, such as a meeting of Commonwealth premiers.

A Parliamentary committee that investigated her activities in the Seventies pointed out that there was a continuing burden of unseen work involving her in hours' of work each day reading/papers in addition to her more public duties.

Secondly, the Queen receives a large number of important people privately. These include those about to be appointed to or retire from senior public posts. She also holds meetings of the Privy Council and around fourteen investitures each year, at which she personally bestows more than 2,000 Orders, declarations and medals.

Thirdly, the Queen attends numerous State occasions, such as the Opening of Parliament, Trooping the Colour, Armistice Day and services at St. Paul's and Westminster Abbey. There are many engagements, both public and private, involving visits to all parts of Britain, such as to universities, hospitals, factories and units of the Armed Forces.

Fourthly, the Queen is directly involved both in State visits to this country of heads of foreign and Commonwealth States. The Parliamentary committee found that the burden had been increasing and saw no sign of it being reduced. When asked by the MPs about her enormous workload, Lord Adeane, then Sir Michael Adeane, her private secretary for nearly twenty years, said: 'I think, to answer this properly, one must divide what the Queen does into certain different bits. First of all her routine work, which is often made much of and is considerable; I do not really think that this has increased a great deal.

'The Commonwealth has increased in size enormously since the Queen has come to the Throne. By that I mean that there are many more units of the Commonwealth with which she is in direct communication. Places which in 1952 she would have dealt with perhaps through the Commonwealth Secretary or in some indirect way, she is now in direct communication with. All this produces a great deal of work. Apart from this the methods of communication, not only getting about herself but making herself seen and heard, have increased and improved very much in the last twenty years.

'I do not think that when the Queen came to the Throne anyone thought of television as being part of what you might describe as the apparatus of Royalty.

'Now it is very much part of it, and one can see, when one goes to some of these rather remote parts of the Commonwealth with the Queen, what the impact of it is, because all sorts of people who would hardly have known that the Queen existed turn out to be as familiar with the everyday life of her family and children and even animals as if they lived in Westminster. So this has all increased.

'When the Queen is actually carrying out engagements the informality, which has become a feature of these things, is a splendid thing and I think it is generally popular. But, of course, in terms of work, which is what you are asking me about, it does enormously increase the work of the Queen.

'In other words, if you go round a selection of 200 people – or not even a selection, just 200 people – and say something to every tenth one or every twentieth one, it is much harder work than merely walking down the middle of the road. This is now expected and this is now done and I am convinced that it is right that it should be done.

'There is one other thing that I think ought to be mentioned in this connection and that is the amount of reading the Queen has to do. Now this is not routine in any sense of the word. This is reading of all sorts, not only familiarising herself with the Government papers which are produced in this country, which she does with great regularity, but keeping fairly well in touch with what is going on in a great many other countries.

'Every day of every year, wherever she is, the Queen receives from her Ministers at home and her representatives in the rest of the Commonwealth and in foreign countries information in the form of telegrams, despatches and letters, as well as submissions, which she has to approve and sign. Her mail consists of an average of 120 letters a day. Thus she can never enjoy a complete holiday. Always at the end of the day there are papers to sign and read, and the Queen is never too tired to deal with them.

'Nobody who does not carry such a burden of responsibility is in a position to appreciate the strain it imposes. The Queen is never absolutely free to do as she likes in the way that ordinary men and women are or to take a holiday. Her job is continuous and she cannot, like other hard-worked people, look forward to a period of retirement at the end of her life.

'Finally it must be remembered that, as well as carrying the exceptional burdens of sovereignty, the Queen carries also those common to all wives and mothers. She must devote time and energy to the upbringing and education of her children and to the care and domestic management of Buckingham Palace, Windsor, Holyroodhouse, Sandringham and Balmoral.

'I very much doubt whether anybody could work more and get more results. I think that the results would begin to go down.'

Would it be possible to reduce the Queen's duties? Sir Michael had an answer to that . . .

'I suppose the whole thing could be done in some totally different way but, assuming that it is done in this way, it would be very difficult to reduce the speed at which the work runs without the results being worse.

'I think that if the Queen gave up reading her papers, people would soon notice that she did not know what was going on; if she refused to go to Australia, the Australians would have a justifiable grievance. You would soon get into trouble over this.'

He went on to say that even with the hardest-working Prince of Wales and Royal Family that there were certain things the Queen herself had to do. 'Nobody realises this more than she does. The Queen knows that she has inherited this particular job. She has a certain future before her and she will undoubtedly go on doing the job to the best of her ability. In a sense you can say, I suppose, that it makes no personal difference to her because she has got to do it anyway.'

Because of the privacy that surrounds the private life of every living monarch, it is impossible to know how the marriage of the Queen and her Consort have fared under the stresses and strains of nearly forty years of marriage. Theirs has to be judged on its public image, carefully processed by a watchful Establishment, but in unguarded moments they seem to be a happy husband and wife. The days when a British monarch could divorce and even execute an unsatisfactory spouse have long since passed.

Prince Philip spoke in Ottawa in 1969 about the future of the Monarchy: 'If the people don't want it, they should change it. But let us end it on amicable terms and not have a row. The Monarchy exists not for its own benefit but for that of the country. We don't come here for our health. We can think of better ways of enjoying ourselves.'

Prince Philip has been Her Majesty's greatest source of strength throughout her Reign – and still is today. His help and advice – and sometimes just his presence at times – are still very much required. To a born leader of men taking second place does not come easily, yet he has always held back a pace or two behind his wife, indicating, with considerable modesty, that she is the ruler and he only her helpmate.

It is, one imagines, an onerous role for someone so forceful in his ways, yet always one notices that he seems, clearly, to be a strong right arm to the Queen. As a mark of her love, affection and respect for him, the Queen made him a Prince of the United Kingdom in 1957, and three years later paid him a greater tribute when she decided to link his own family name of Mountbatten forever with that of the British Royal Line.

Eleven days before the birth of Prince Andrew, she declared 'In Council' on 8 February 1960: 'While I and my children shall continue to be styled and known as the House and Family of Windsor, my descendants, other than descendants enjoying the style, title or attributes of Royal Highness and the titular dignity of Prince or Princess and female descendants who marry and their descendants, shall bear the name Mountbatten-Windsor.'

An explanatory statement went on to say: 'The Queen has always wanted, without changing the name of the Royal House established by her grandfather, to associate the name of her husband with her own and his descendants. The Queen has had this in mind for a long time and it is close to her heart.'

Philip is a Prince but not a 'Prince Consort', sharing the power of the Throne. He has never wanted this. He is never invited to look at State papers and takes no part in the official running of the State. His lack of any official status has given him a greater freedom than any other senior member of the Royal Family has enjoyed. Consequently, he has enthusiastically dedicated himself to a variety of organisations ranging from the World Wildlife Fund to his own highly successful Duke of Edinburgh's Award Scheme, which has encouraged thousands of teenagers to try to attain excellence in hundreds of activities.

The Queen has invariably given way to Philip where personal or family matters are concerned. 'Ask Papa,' is what she says to their children, or to friends, 'I'll ask Philip.' She is Head of State, Church and Commonwealth, but at home Philip is master of the house.

Philip's former headmaster at Gordonstoun, Kurt Hahn, once wrote of him: 'Prince Philip is a born leader but will need the exacting demands of a great service to do justice to himself. His best is outstanding; his second best is not good enough. Prince Philip will make his mark in any profession where he will have to prove himself in a trial of strength.'

He has truly lived up to these expectations. His strength has frequently been put on trial in the service of the Queen, and he has never failed her.

ALL THE ROYAL FAMILY are keen on horses but Her Majesty has a particularly enthusiastic interest. Her main hobby is both breeding and racing horses, and her devotion to it almost borders on the obsessional. Her equine activities began early in life helped along by the fact that her father's string of racehorses won so often. When he died she inherited not only his two stud stables in Norfolk but also his spirit for the sport.

The story goes that on the eve of her Coronation a lady-in-waiting said to her, 'You must be feeling apprehensive, Ma'am,' and the Queen is said to have replied, 'Yes, but I'm sure my horse will still win.' Her horse was Aureole, a worthy animal that came second in the Derby a few days after her Crowning.

She has four stables where she breeds and trains, keeping a close eye on the programme. In addition to the breeding, she has twenty to thirty thoroughbreds in training which, between them, usually bring in a substantial amount of money each year. Such is her skill as an expert on pedigrees that over the last twenty-five years she is estimated to have picked up more than a million pounds in prize money.

The Queen has had nearly 350 winners to date. In 1954 she became the first British monarch since Charles II to head the list of winning owners.

As Princess Elizabeth, she started in partnership with the Queen Mother when, in 1949, they bought an Irish bred steeplechaser called Monaveen for £1,000 on the recommendation of Royal trainer, Peter Cazalet. Monaveen used to pull an Irish milk float and had once changed hands for £35. On his first outing in Royal Colours at Fontwell Park he won with ease by fifteen lengths. He was destroyed after breaking a leg at the water jump while lying second in the £2,000 Queen Elizabeth Chase at Hurst Park at the beginning of December 1950.

Elizabeth was so upset that she gave up as an owner for a while, and she has never been fond of steeplechasing since then. She became an owner again at the time of her Coronation with Aureole as a firm favourite. By the time he retired to stud at Sandringham, where the Queen frequently went to talk to him in his stable, he had won £36,225 in two years. Lord Porchester, the Queen's racing manager, says: 'Our aim is to make the risky game of breeding as much of a self-financing exercise as possible.'

She still has not had a Derby winner, even though, as her jockey, Willie Carson once said, 'You feel a bit different when you put on the Royal Colours – a little more important, and your adrenalin gets going quicker. But it doesn't make the horses go any faster.'

Prince Charles, speaking to a group of businessmen, once said: 'Whenever I back one of my mother's horses, it is always a total disaster. I keep well out of that and I advise you to do the same thing.' His advice was bad on this occasion – a few days later one of them romped home at 3-1.

One of her best years was 1974, when she won her first classic race for sixteen years with Highclere's victory in the One Thousand Guineas. The horse went on to win Le Prix de Diane – the French Oaks – rounding off her total winnings for the year to nearly £140,000.

The Queen is a wealth of knowledge on horses and their ways, and it is this understanding perhaps that explains her fearlessness when she is around them. Nowhere was this more dramatically demonstrated than at the Royal Windsor Horse Show in May 1978 when she stopped a runaway four-horse team. The incident was described afterwards by the leader of four Household Cavalry soldiers manning the coach. Captain Nicholas d'Ambrumenil: 'We hit a bank after going past the third obstacle and were all turfed out. We attempted to chase the horses for several hundred yards and then I saw the Queen step forward to shout 'Whoa!' and take hold of the reins.

'Then Prince Philip came up and they both quietened the animals while the carriage was put back.' Captain d'Ambrumenil said the horses were going at a 'fair pace' when they bolted with the carriage. 'We were having quite a job keeping up with them before the Queen stopped them.'

The Queen had been watching the race from a Land Rover with Prince Philip. An eyewitness said: 'Neither the Queen nor Prince Philip hesitated for a moment when they saw the runaway horses. They dashed out in front of them. The Queen was waving her arms and Prince Philip grabbed for the bridle of the leading horse.' Later Prince Philip successfully negotiated the tricky course without error with the Queen's team of bay geldings.

HER LOVE OF creatures large and small is such that she was particularly upset when Irish terrorists not only attacked and killed her own troopers with a bomb attack on the Household Cavalry in Hyde Park in July 1982, but also killed and injured many horses.

Four troopers died and seven horses destroyed when the IRA bomb exploded as the Blues and Royals Regiment, carrying their standard, rode past. The explosion was heard at Buckingham Palace.

The most famous of the equine injured was Sefton, a twenty-year-old bandsman's mount, who suffered some of the worst wounds, yet pulled through. She was especially interested in looking out for him back on parade almost a year later when the Queen remembered the brave troopers of the Household Cavalry as she presented new standards to the regiment on Horse Guards' Parade.

During the ceremony the Queen, who is their Colonel-in-Chief, commented on the tattered scarlet and gold standard which had just been carried from the Parade Ground... a poignant memento of the attack. 'In the midst of this pageantry, for want of a better word, there could be no more timely or honourable reminder, to those of us who need reminding, that the soldier's life is never free of danger.'

Some of the men injured in the bombing were on that special parade, as were horses which survived the attack. Sefton, still showing the scars of his injuries, walked in the band that day.

It was a proud and colourful occasion. The Guards, looking magnificent in their uniforms of scarlet, blue and gold, trooped before the Queen, their plumes of white and scarlet catching the brisk breeze, harnesses jingling and hooves clattering on the gravel. And as a gesture the world took to be a mark of contempt for the callous killers, the Queen rode there in an open carriage once used by Queen Victoria, despite fears for her safety.

After a service of consecration before more than 600 men, the Queen moved from her dais to hand to their commanding officers the eight new standards, four for the Life Guards and four for the Blues and Royals. Finally, the cavalry and the band set off at a brisk trot around the parade ground.

They were followed by armoured cars and tanks, which lowered their guns in salute as they passed the Queen, who was accompanied by Princess Anne.

Animals have always figured prominently in her life, indeed the whole family's fondness for dogs goes back several generations. Queen Victoria so loved them that she owned eighty-three at the time of her death. When his favourite Irish terrier died, Edward VII had some of its hair made into a bracelet. His wife, Queen Alexandra, kept so many pets at Buckingham Palace that her successor, Queen Mary, would not have a dog in the place – except for George V's cairn terriers, first Snip, then Bob, who took the King his morning paper.

Edward VIII, the Duke of Windsor, was also fond of cairn terriers. He carried Slipper under his arm when he boarded the Naval destroyer that took him into exile.

Those ankle-snapping, noisy, Royal corgis have been around, of course, since 1933 when the Duke and Duchess of York bought Elizabeth a puppy and called him Dookie. He sired Crackers and Carol, from whom the rest were bred. At five o'clock every afternoon when she is at home the Queen feeds her corgis, distributing the food into several bowls with a silver fork and spoon.

Mere mortals have one birthday each year. The Queen has two – her natural anniversary and, by tradition, an official birthday that can be celebrated, hopefully, in the June sunshine. This is marked by a glittering ceremony, a review of the Household Troops, known the world over as Trooping the Colour. It is an almost sacred occasion for the foot and mounted guards – the elite of the British Army – as they march and counter-march or trot before their Sovereign who, sitting sidesaddle on a magnificantly turned-out horse, returns their display with a salute.

The Sovereign's Birthday Parade dates from the 19th Century, although its origins stretch back to the time when flags or 'colours' were used as rallying points for troops in battle. After each day's march it would be carried, or 'trooped', down the ranks to ensure that every fighting man – usually illiterate, and often a mercenary who did not speak English – could recognise his regimental flag.

The Queen arrives on horseback from Buckingham Palace at exactly 11 am watched by the Queen Mother and other members of the Royal Family from an upper window. Usually she is accompanied by Prince Philip, Prince Charles and her cousin, the Duke of Kent. Then it all begins. She is received with a Royal Salute, with the bands playing the National Anthem.

After the last note has faded away on the soft June air she inspects the parade, riding the full length of the ranks and returning to the saluting base. The colour is then trooped from left to right down the line of guards, to the sound of *'The Grenadiers' March'*. Next it is the turn of the Household Cavalry, who ride line abreast, dipping the standard as each troop passes the Queen.

The ceremony ends with the march back up the Mall to Buckingham Palace, the Queen at the head of her guards, followed by Prince Philip. While the column assembles at the Queen Victoria Memorial, the Royal Procession enters the Palace forecourt in preparation for a final march past by the footguards and mounted bands, followed by jets of RAF Strike Command flying over Buckingham Palace. By then the Queen has joined the rest of her family on the balcony.

An indication of how the Queen was planning her Sixtieth Birthday Celebrations could be guessed from similar festivities ten years ago. Then, she celebrated her Fiftieth Birthday in a style thought by many to have long gone. On the eve of the big day 1,000 guests were invited to a dance at Windsor Castle. It took place in the Waterloo Chamber and long gallery of St George's hall, to the merry clink of champagne glasses and music, and cost more than £5,000, paid for by the Queen.

☆*Star-note. The Queen's birth sign is Taurus. According to astrologers she seems to have all the characteristics of a Taurean woman ... she is emotional, has a loving nature, is courageous but exercises self-restraint, displays loyalty and has a reassuring straightforwardness.*

AS STRANGE AS it may seem to a housewife who feels she spends her entire life looking after a home and family, the Queen, in her own way, also runs a 'home' – or, in her case, several homes. Plenty of servants, yes, but decisions still have to be made about where the meat is bought, who delivers the bread and butter, and where the best buys can be found for everything from shoes to raincoats, bananas to baubles.

The Queen, with the help of her staff, decides who shall be given the privilege of delivering the groceries, and other items on her shopping list, to the Royal palaces. Those chosen are allowed to display on their shop doors and letterheadings a crown, signifying they are Royal Warrant Holders.

There are so many of them that they have their own association, founded in 1840. It used to be a gathering of 'Her Majesty's Tradesmen', who met every year on May, 25 Queen Victoria's birthday. Today the Royal Warrant Holders' Association, which dates back to 1907, makes sure there is no imitation or wrongful use of the Royal Coat of Arms and that the warrant-holding members of the association abide by the rules governing them. It also takes steps to protect the use of the Royal Arms under the Trade Marks Act and the Trade Descriptions Act.

The rules of the association state that the warrant 'is a mark of recognition that an individual is a supplier of goods or services to the Royal Household.' It allows the lucky tradesman to use the term 'By Appointment' and to display the Royal Coat of Arms on his company's products, as well on his premises and on stationery and other printed material, such as shopping bags and advertisements.

Among them are Spink & Son Limited of King Street, London SW1, who are medallists to HM The Queen, HRH The Duke of Edinburgh and HRH The Prince of Wales. They design and make orders, decorations and medals, renovate medals, replace lost ones and advise when, where and how to wear medals . .

THE Crown Jewellers *par excellence,* however, are Garrard & Company Limited of Regent Street, London W1. Their connection with the Royal Family dates back to their beginnings in 1722. Among the recent commissions taken on by Garrard's was the engagement ring for the Princess of Wales.

There is also Cartier Limited of New Bond Street, London W1, who started as jewellers and goldsmiths in 1847 when Louis-François set up business in Paris. They invented the clip brooch ... Asprey & Company, also of New Bond Street, started by William Asprey, a Huguenot,

over 200 years ago, are other Royal gemsmiths.
Collingwood Limited of Conduit Street, London W1 are also jewellers and silversmiths to the Queen and have been involved with Royal weddings for more than 100 years. They made the wedding band for the Princess of Wales. Toye, Kenning & Spencer Limited of Great Queen Street, London WC2 supply gold and silver laces, insignia and embroidery to the Queen. They also weave messages across sweatshirts, ties, badges, shields, spoons, medals and key rings...

Then there is Stuart Devlin Limited of St. John Street, London EC1 – a young Australian goldsmith who is said to turn 'everything he touches to gold'. from the smallest paperweight to the most spectacular candelabra. Buttons come from Firmin & Sons PLC of Crawford Street, London W1. Their buttons were worn by Wellington's men at Waterloo – 'and probably by Napoleon's too', say some wits.

When the Queen has a garden party she uses Black & Edgington of Queen Elizabeth Street, Tower Bridge, London SE1 to provide the tents and flags. They have held their Royal Warrant since Queen Victoria's day. Food at a Royal 'do' in one of the gardens can be supplied by such people as Crawfords Catering of Distillery Lane, Edinburgh, who are Caterers to HM The Queen. Their menus include quails' eggs in aspic jelly, *suprème of chicken chaud froid* and fresh pears poached in port. They have more than fifty years' experience of looking after the stately stomachs of England!

Royal swords for knighting come from Wilkinson Sword Limited of Brunel Road, London W3. They go back to 1772 and today of course also do a brisk business in razor blades. Boots and shoes are made by Henry Maxwell & Company Limited of Savile Row, London W1, James North & Sons Limited of Hyde, Cheshire, and, more often than not, by John Lobb Limited of St. James's Street, London SW1.

Robes for State occasions are usually tailored by Ede & Ravenscroft Limited of Chancery Lane, London WC2. They even gowned Queen Victoria for her Coronation. Half their trade today is export, designing and making robes for African chiefs, new universities and foreign dignitaries. They were established in 1689 and they have been robe-makers to every English Monarch since that year.

The world-famous Harrods and Fortnum and Mason supply the Royal groceries, and if the Queen really wants to make a grand finale of her entertaining, she even has firework makers 'By Royal Appointment'. They are Kimbolton Fireworks of High Street, Kimbolton, Huntingdon, Cambridgeshire, which is run by a vicar, the Reverend Lancaster, who designed displays for the Queen's Silver Jubilee.

HOW THE QUEEN RULES

HER MAJESTY rules by the rights of a constitution that goes back eleven centuries. The Monarchy is the oldest secular institution in Britain, tracing its origins to 829 AD: that was the year the Saxon King Egbert united England when he became King of Wessex and All England. The Queen descends from Egbert, who reigned for twelve years.

According to some genealogists, the Royal Family can also claim in its ancestry the Prophet of Islam, Mohammed, and the first President of the United States, George Washington. As well as being related to almost every past and present royal family in Europe for over 150 years – thanks to the prolific breeding of Queen Victoria – the Queen and her children also include a few ordinary Smiths and Browns in their backgrounds.

Until the First World War the family belonged to the House of Saxe-Coburg and Gotha, a link with Queen Victoria's prince consort who was Prince Albert of Saxe-Coburg and Gotha. Feelings were running so high against Germany during the war that King George V made a proclamation in 1917 that Windsor would be the family name of all Queen Victoria's male descendants, and in April 1952, before her Coronation, Queen Elizabeth II declared that she and all her children should be known as the House and Family of Windsor.

The Monarchy is four centuries older than Parliament and three centuries older than the British judicial system. Its continuity has been broken only once – that was eleven years from 1649 to 1660, when Britain was governed by Oliver Cromwell.

Up to the end of the Seventeenth Century, when Parliament established a monarchy with limited rights, Queen Elizabeth's predecessors personally exercised supreme executive, legislative and judicial powers. By the end of the last century all the Sovereign's political power was terminated and the Queen must now accede to Parliament's wishes and be an impartial head of State.

Her Majesty's power, such as it is, is limited by the constitution. She may use her discretion on two occasions: the appointment of a Prime Minister and the Dissolution of Parliament. Before a General Election is called, it is she who dissolves the last Parliament. When the leader of the winning party is elected, it is Her Majesty who appoints him her Prime Minister.

Every year, she opens each new session of Parliament. Her Address from the Throne, outlining in the House of Lords the proposed legislation in the following year, is known as the Queen's Speech, although it is actually written by the Prime Minister.

Over the years, the powers of the Monarchy have been almost entirely done away with. The first Queen Elizabeth actually ruled the country. In an emergency she commanded the Navy to put to sea and the Army to fight. Today, although Queen Elizabeth II is Lord High Admiral and Head of the Armed Forces, she has no authority to do the same. Despite this, there is the formality that any Government still has to get the Royal assent before using the Armed Forces in a major military conflict. All Servicemen swear allegiance to the Crown – not the Government.

Her Privy Council is the highest formal institution of government in the land. The Queen 'In Council' is still required to give formal approval to orders and proclamations, using powers given by Acts of Parliament. All members of the Cabinet automatically become Councillors and they are appointed for life.

An indication of how a Privy Councillor behaves and is dealt with by Her Majesty was given by the former Socialist minister, the late Richard Crossman. He recalled that on his first visit to Buckingham Palace for a council meeting he decided that the Queen was shy. 'If one waits for her to begin the conversation, nothing happens.'

At Sandringham in January 1967 Mr. Crossman attended a Privy Council. The Queen told him she felt a great deal more remote from London than at Balmoral. 'They all love this place because it was Edward VII's hideout and has become a family hideout where they can feel more like ordinary human beings.'

After an afternoon walk he found the Queen doing an enormous and difficult jigsaw. 'Her lady-in-waiting told me she was jolly good at jigsaws and, sure enough, while she was standing there talking to the company at large, her fingers were straying and she was quietly fitting in the pieces while apparently not looking round.'

After a period of apprenticeship Mr. Crossman began to realise that it was inconsiderate to expect the Queen to offer even the mildest political comment. Constitutionally she was politically neutral and this could often place her in invidious positions.

As an example, after a Privy Council at Windsor in November 1967, four councillors, all members of the Labour Government, adjourned with the Queen to the television room to watch a broadcast by the Prime Minister, Harold Wilson. As he sat on the sofa with the Queen, Mr. Crossman thought, 'What on earth are we to say to each other when the broadcast finishes?'

In theory, the Queen could bring the machinery of government to a halt by ignoring Ministerial advice and refusing to give her consent to Government policy. In reality, she would not dare to exercise the Royal Prerogative.

She still has the duty to step in, though, if a government resigns without calling a General Election – therefore leaving the political life of the nation in limbo. She could appoint the leader of the next largest party or ask the Prime Minister to stay on until a successor was elected. She could choose a successor herself or encourage a coalition. The Queen could also dissolve Parliament against the wishes of a Prime Minister who had been defeated in a vote of confidence, but had refused to resign or ask for a dissolution.

Although there are a number of Acts, as well as common law rules of descent, giving her the right to rule, the Queen stays on the Throne essentially by the consent of her people. If the majority of her subjects turned against both her and the monarchial system, there could be pressure through parliament to end the Windsor Dynasty: a prospect that seems highly unlikely in an era when the British Royal Family is the strongest and most popularly supported of any of the monarchies which remain in a world of republicanism.

QUEEN ELIZABETH II rules at a time of changing attitudes towards monarchies everywhere. She realises well enough that the days of an aloof monarch on a golden throne are over. With this in mind, over the past thirty-four years she has tried to become closer to the people. In order to know how people live and cope with the problems of their lives, the Royal Family has kept in step with the developments in the streets outside its palaces and castles.

The Monarchy has survived during the last three hundred years by adroitly adjusting to changing times. The Queen has shown the same adaptive speed in the changes that have been apparent during her lifetime. Her father was the last King Emperor of India, yet in 1961 she was able to return to India and Pakistan and receive the sort of welcome that perhaps could never have been the case had Britain hung on to her rule.

During the early part of her reign, the Queen was pre-eminently the Head of the Commonwealth and, in the course of these duties, became the most travelled monarch in history. She is dedicated to the unity of the Commonwealth, to the service of all – not any section or class or group.

To the millions of citizens of the Commonwealth Elizabeth represents unity, dignity and the simple virtues of a good family life. She is a national image to the world. The Commonwealth is the inner core of her faith in her office. She feels that her supreme service at this moment in history is to hold it together. She and Prince Philip are both prepared to make any effort in the way of State or private visits in pursuit of this ideal.

As a link between Commonwealth countries, as well as between the races forming their internal 'ethnic' populations, the Queen's symbolic position is unique. She unifies because she is above suspicion and corruption.

Elizabeth likes to think there is a family spirit about the Commonwealth, where everyone feels they know each other, that they have something in common. These come about from a common language, common culture, common experience and common history. Thanks to several Acts of Parliament in Australia, Canada and New Zealand, the Queen is also just as much 'owned' by these nations as she is the Queen of Great Britain.

As Prince Charles said on one occasion at a gathering of Commonwealth youth: 'I believe that the Queen, as head of the Commonwealth, is an important part of keeping the whole thing together.' There is plenty of evidence that the Queen brings to her job not only great industry and conscientiousness but a dispassionate sense of judgment.

Her role as a politically neutral adviser to prime ministers is vital. On this matter she does her homework. Lord Wilson of Rievaulx, formerly Sir Harold Wilson, made sure that he had read all relevant State Papers before meeting the Queen: 'If she quoted one I hadn't yet read, I felt like a schoolboy who hadn't done his homework.'

At the time of the Queen's Silver Jubilee he said: 'You realise very quickly that she is a unique repository of knowledge ... and what emerges is a combination of experience, very hard work, a good memory and good judgment, both about things and people. If we in Britain had been governed for hundreds of years by a presidential system, the best constitutional innovation for modern times would be to invent a sovereign.'

Another ex-premier, Lord Home – as Sir Alec Douglas-Home he was at No. 10 in 1963 – once paid this tribute: 'The Queen knows almost every head of state and leader of government in foreign countries, while, as head of the Commonwealth, she has an intimate knowledge of the leading personalities and of their ways. Her experience is readily put at the disposal of the Prime Minister and is invaluable to him. She is always up to date and fully versed in the niceties of every national and international problem.'

Indeed, she must now be ranked not only as one of the senior figures on the world stage but also as among the most respected. Since she came to the Throne, she has outlasted seven British Prime Ministers, six US Presidents, six power changes in Russia, three Popes and countless French and Italian Governments. Her reign also has seen the deaths of such historical figures as Sir Winston Churchill, President John Kennedy, De Gaulle, Franco, Chiang Kai-shek, Haile Selassie, Mao Tse-tung and Marshal Tito.

Britain has gone through many social, political and industrial revolutions in recent decades ... the loss of world power and empire, the entry into the EEC, changes in education and the social services, financial crises and a war in the South Atlantic. During these events the stability of the Monarchy, and the continued presence of the Queen, has been a reassuring anchor to cling to in the headlong rush.

There has been talk in some – non-Royal – circles of abdication. The Queen sees herself as a lady only halfway through her career. She intends to remain there as long as she retains her physical strength and the affection of her people. As years go by, she is expected to unload more of her burdens on to Charles. Abdication is out – at least for many years to come. It would be a mistake and a waste. For the value of a well-trained constitutional monarch to the nation tends to increase as the reign lengthens.

Prince Charles, now aged thirty-seven, dismissed suggestions that his mother should soon give up the Throne in his favour. He sees no reason why she should retire. He feels that, because of the vast constitutional and political knowledge a monarch acquires by the time he or she reaches normal retirement age, the sovereign is then at a 'most useful stage'. If the Queen lives to the ages of her mother, grandmother or great-great-grandmother Queen Victoria – eighty two – it could be the beginning of the twenty-first century before Charles reaches the Throne.

Happily, the Queen is still a healthy woman, immersed in her job and as deeply interested as ever in the affairs of State. A youthful king could be popular, though, both at home and abroad. Lord Home again: 'It would create a very dangerous and undesirable precedent if the Queen were to abdicate. Once is enough.

'As a newly married man with a young family, Charles should be allowed to enjoy his private life now. There will be plenty of time for him to learn the craft of monarchy later.'

As a Palace aide explained: 'Don't expect any sweeping changes in Prince Charles's career, but as the Queen gets older he'll gradually take over more of her functions, particularly the overseas touring. Under the British system abdication doesn't happen. The Monarch remains Monarch for life.'

Quipped another of Her Majesty's long serving courtiers on this subject; "We have beheaded monarchs, usurped monarchs, but we do not have retired monarchs!"

The Government and Her Majesty's constitutional advisers point out as well that it is only in countries like Holland and Belgium that a sovereign 'retires.' She is still the head of a family that symbolises all that is best about Britain. It is also a focus for all the pageantry and spectacle of the nation. At her sixtieth birthday, the Queen is as dedicated as ever she was to the task she inherited thirty-four years ago.

At her Silver Jubilee celebrations in London's Guildhall, the Queen recalled the pledge she had made so many years earlier. 'When I was twenty-one, I pledged my life to the service of our people and I asked for God's help to make good that vow. Although that vow was made in my salad days when I was green in judgement, I do not regret or retract one word of it.'

LONG MAY SHE REIGN.

THE COLOURFUL
MOMENTS
HER MAJESTY
WILL
REMEMBER...

The War years, 1941, at Windsor Castle with her mother the Queen and young sister Margaret.

A young Princess with a fairytale future, reflects by the lake at Buckingham Palace in 1946. Above, a rare family picture with her parents and sister.

Above, a most relaxed mood for Princess Elizabeth and (right) a more formal picture of Princess Elizabeth wearing a white satin dress embroidered with crystals and pearls and the Russian Fringe Tiara, taken in the White Drawing Room at Buckingham Palace.

The young Princess at her desk at Buckingham Palace.

A beautiful study of young Princess Elizabeth at Buckingham Palace (left) and above, The Royal Family at Balmoral in 1952.

Her Majesty's marriage to the Duke of Edinburgh, 1947 (left) and (above) the wedding of Prince Charles and Lady Diana Spencer.

The group photograph at the wedding of Her Majesty The Queen.

The Queen and Prince Philip, the man who has been at her side since 1947.

A place of pride in the family album – the day Master Peter Phillips, son of Princess Anne

and Captain Mark Phillips, visited his grandparents and uncles at Buckingham Palace.

The engagement of the Prince of Wales to Lady Diana Spencer was announced in February 1981. The happy couple were photographed in the gardens of Buckingham Palace.

The Duchess of York, with Princess Elizabeth and Princess Margaret (left) at The Royal Lodge, Windsor, in June 1936 and (above) The Queen and Prince Philip with their younger sons, Prince Andrew and Prince Edward in 1975.

The Queen and Her family on the balcony of Buckingham Palace after Trooping the Colour.

King George VI and his family enjoy a Sunday

afternoon at Royal Lodge, Windsor, in 1946.

The Prince and The Princess of Wales' honeymoon started when they boarded the Royal Yacht Britannia in Gibraltar... and ended at Balmoral Castle.

HER MAJESTY AT SIXTY